READER ANALYSIS OF THE EPISTLE OF JAMES

RANDALL C. WEBBER

READER RESPONSE
ANALYSIS OF
THE EPISTLE OF JAMES

RANDALL C. WEBBER

International Scholars Publications
San Francisco - London - Bethesda
1996

Library of Congress Cataloging-in-Publication Data

Webber, Randall C., 1961-
  Reader response analysis of the Epistle of James / Randall C.
  Webber.
    p. cm.
  Includes bibliographical references and indexes.
  ISBN 1-57292-087-5 (cloth : alk. paper). -- ISBN 1-57292-086-7 (pbk. :
  alk. paper)
  1. Bible. N.T. James—Criticism, interpretation, etc. 2. Reader
  -response criticism. I. Title.
  BS2785.2.W43   1996
  227'.9106—dc20   96-33536
                                                              CIP

Editorial Inquiries:
Austin & Winfield, Publishers
7831 Woodmont Avenue #345
Bethesda, MD 20814
(301) 654-7335

To Order: (800) 99-AUSTIN

CONTENTS

Acknowledgements   iii

Chapter 1
Reading James: Equivocation and Polyvalence   1

    Reading Strategy: A Social Model   3

    Social Characteristics of Modern Readings of James   15

    The Polyvalent Character of James   22

Chapter 2
James in Classical Antiquity: Some General Considerations   31

    The Author's Identity   33

    The Epistle in Its Cultural Milieu   38

    The Addressees Within the Recipient Churches   54

i

Chapter 3

James in a Hypothetical, Post-Pauline Milieu   59

    A Post-Pauline Reading of James   65

        Testing and Perseverence   67

        Wisdom   73

        Economic Favoritism   80

        Verbal Riposte   87

    James, Paul, and Abraham   92

Chapter 4

Epilogue: James in Diverse Settings   95

    James in a Hypothetical, Palestinian Provenance   99

    James in Canonical Context   105

Works Cited   109

Index to ancient writings   117

General index   123

ACKNOWLEDGEMENTS

The author expresses appreciation for the assistance of numerous individuals in the preparation of this work. Ann Taves and her panel at the 1995 American Academy of Religion meeting led a meeting on transforming dissertations into books which proved equally informative in the composition from scratch of this monograph. Gary Millsaps of Lyndon Baptist Church and Brooke Webber proofread the manuscript in its entirety and suggested many revisions to improve clarity and readability. Bill Londrigan and Joe Wise of the Greater Louisville Building Trades Council, AFL-CIO, provided scanning equipment and expertise to recover a chapter lost inadvertently at a late stage of the game. Finally, Robert West of International Scholars Publications provided advice and encouragement regarding legal and mechanical matters throughout the composition and publication process.

Institutions, like the individuals noted above, provided extensive assistance throughout the writing and publication process. The Louisville Presbyterian Theological Seminary, the Southern Baptist Theological Seminary, and the University of Louisville made all resources in their libraries, including some items from their rare book collections, available to the author without hesitation. Their employees performed consistently in a courteous and knowledgable manner. Compaq Computer, Hewlett-Packard, amd Microsoft must receive credit for the especially reliable performance of their low-end computer, printer, and software. The Veteran's Administration chaplaincy department, the Salvation Army Center of Hope, and their clients and employees provided many helpful suggestions at various points.

I would be remiss in neglecting the contributions of three groups to this project. The material on James began as a training handbook for the adult Sunday School teachers of Lyndon Baptist Church, Louisville, KY. Their comments and suggestions provided much food for thought during the preparation of this more academic work. The material on James was analyzed in terms of a social model of reading developed for use with the Apocalyse; I am grateful to the Reading the Apocalypse Group of the Society of Biblical Literature for its encouragement of this line of thought and its constructive criticism of both the model and its initial application to the apocalypse. Finally, the Social Sciences and New Testament Section of the Society of Biblical Literature provided a substantial volume of literature regarding the social and anthropological theories appropriate to the inhabitants of the eastern Mediterranean basin during the first century CE. Its recent attempts to relate such theories to the literary characteristics of the writings under examination also proved enlightening.

My final debt is to the reader. All remaining errors, omissions, unclear aspects of presentation, and weaknesses of argument remain my sole responsibility. It is by careful consideration of the following presentation's advantages and drawbacks and by drawing and publishing your own conclusions that you will advance the state of knowledge about this much neglected Christian writing: In a figurative sense, "become doers of the word rather than merely listeners who delude themselves" (James 1:22).

RCW
Louisville, KY, USA
7/4/96

iv

Chapter One

READING JAMES:
EQUIVOCATION AND POLYVALENCE

Christian audiences have received the Epistle to James equivocally throughout its existence. The epistle's acceptance as an authoritative Christian writing occurred late in the canonization process. Since the fourth century anthologist Eusebius noted the scarcity of direct citations of James (HE 3:23-25), the canonization process probably reflected a preceding pattern of misgivings. Luther's well-known reference to James as "an epistle of straw," a derogatory comparison with the Pauline corpus by means of allusion to 1 Cor. 3:10-15, exaggerated rather than misrepresented the earlier pattern of Christian misgivings about James. Luther's interpretaton of Paul, of course, has influenced the modern Protestant canon within the canon to a considerable extent. Since James includes much seemingly useful ethical instruction, the reasons for its equivocal usage by ante-Nicene Christians are not completely certain.

Likewise, the reasons for the ultimate canonization of the epistle remain far from lucid. James, though canonical, seems to contradict major tenets of the post-Pauline tradition which came to define Christian orthodoxy. The author disputes a doctrine of justification by faith, emphasizes ethical behavior in a manner seemingly foreign to Paul and his successors, attacks apparently parasitical but socially informed behavior by potentially influential church members, and prescribes confession and healing rituals which were possibly but not necessarily comparable to the practices of other early Christian communities.

Extant evidence regarding the circulation of James supports Eusebius' contention that his predecessors cited the epistle infrequently, at least as a widely

1

accepted writing. J. B. Mayor catalogues the Jacobin citations/allusions extant from the first three centuries.[1] Most of these selections display similarities at the level of terminology, phraseology, and imagery in brief passages, so Mayor's uncritical acceptance of the passages as evidence that James was well-known is anachronistic. However, Mayor's illustration of the sheer volume of similarities leads to the following two positive conclusions regarding the early circulation of James: First, the large quantity of relevant ante-Nicene passages, possibly analogous to circumstantial evidence in forensic settings, suggests that the similarities were not accidental, in other words, that James enjoyed wide distribution in Christian circles. Second, in most cases, if or when ante-Nicene Christian writers referred to the epistle, they did so without citing it explicitly as one of their widely, though informally (at that time), accepted writings.

The consistently paraphrastic reference to James or similar tradition contrasts sharply with the more explicit manner in which Christians cited their scriptures in many instances, though not exclusively. Few NT writers were reluctant to quote relevant passages from the Septuagint (LXX) directly and at length. In addition, the synoptic authors portrayed a Jesus who recognized the law and prophets, at least, as authoritative and contrasted them with human traditions (e.g., Matt. 22:40 also Mk. 7:1-13, 12:18-34, Lk. 10:25-28, 18:18-23). The author of 2 Peter noted the existence of a collection of Paul's letters (3:14-16). Eusebius cited the no longer extant Papias (early second century) as recognizing a gospel, presumably an accepted account of Jesus' life, written by Mark on the basis of Peter's recollections and also a collection of dominical oracles in Hebrew or Aramaic and associated with the name of Matthew (HE:3:39:14-17). The cross-fertilization of James and other Christian and Jewish traditions of the first three centuries is highly probable and assumed for purposes of this study, given the volume of references. However the consistently brief and paraphrastic character of the references before Origen (c. 253 CE) sets James apart from the mainstays of the emerging collections of Hebrew and Christian scripture which became the Christian canon in subsequent centuries.

---

[1] *The Epistle of James*, 2nd ed. (London/New York: MacMillan, 1897), pp. li-lxviii.

The intersection of traditions establishes a point of departure for this study. Mayor traces the fate of James in terms of his own concept of the canonization process. In Mayor's thought, the canonization process received its definitive impetus from the churches of the western Mediterranean basin, particularly those at Rome and Carthage, though the influence of the eastern churches could not be denied. James circulated primarily in the eastern Mediterranean basin because it was addressed to Jewish Christians in that area.[2] Consequently, James appears on most of the eastern and few of the western lists of accepted Christian writings before the time of Augustine and Jerome. Actually, the early ecumenical councils ratified canonical lists proposed by bishops of eastern provenance, such as Athanasius, Antilochius and Cyril of Jerusalem, all of which included James. Thus the lists of the mid-fourth century CE support at least the one side of Mayor's argument regarding the eastern Mediterranean provenance of James.

This study examines both the equivocation and the ultimate acceptance of the epistle of James by the Christian successors to the Pauline tradition. It develops a reader-oriented model of literary interpretation, uses both culturally specific and cross-cultural data as checks and balances on interpretation, and grounds the model firmly in a theory of the social dimensions of knowledge. The study tests this model by constructing two hypothetical, late first century CE audiences for James and interpreting the epistle in terms which such audiences might find familiar. Since data outside of the epistle itself provide the bulk of the material for audience construction, this approach limits, though it does not eliminate, the circular aspects inherent in the analysis of ancient literature.

Reading Strategy: A Social Model

As nascent Christianity began to develop institutional forms, pharasaic Judaism underwent a comparable process. The *tannaim* developed a tradition of halakhic refinement of the legal prescriptions of the Hebrew scriptures. This tradition applied existing ethical norms from the Hebrew scriptures to more recent

---

[2]Mayor, *Epistle of James*, p. li.

circumstances; in this respect, the tradition performed in a more thorough manner the function which James served among its listeners. The *tannaim* preserved this tradition in the form of contrasting positions on various issues, arranged as scholarly, most likely artificial, debates among rabbis of comparable provenance and reputation. The Hebrew canon (c. 90 CE), Mishnah (c. 200), Jerusalem Talmud (c. 400), and Babylonian Talmud (c. 600) provide examples of this tradition at four separate times. The time frame for the development of the halakhic tradition is longer than that for the initial developments within Christianity, but the concept of conscious and intentional accountability to a (fictive?) community of peers, the definitive factor in the development of the tradition, provides a suitable point of departure for the development of a more general description of a manner in which interpretation may become institutionalized. Such accountability dictates that one analyze community and literature in terms of their interrelationship, insofar as the data may permit.

The *tannaim* began to codify their traditions in response to the social upheaval forced upon them by two abortive uprisings against Rome. The hostilities of 66-73 CE eradicated most of the groups indigenous to Jerusalem and left a cultural, political, and religious vacuum among Palestinian Jews. Since the predecessors of the *tannaim* enjoyed fairly broad geographic support, their position was conducive to survival after the hostilities moved to Jerusalem for their climax. The Bar Kochba revolt some 65 years later completed this process, forced Roman troops to raze Jerusalem and restablish the city as a Roman colony, and left the *tannaim* in Galilee as the only group with sufficient intellectual and organizational capacity to forge any sort of Palestinian Jewish identity.[3]

The *tannaim* initiated a process of literary development which influences even the character of present-day Jewish faith and practice. Within a generation after the revolt of 66-73 CE, they established the masoretic text of the current 39 books as normative to bring to its culmination a process which even some contemporaneous Christian compositions acknowledged by reference to the law,

---

[3]M. Goodman, *State and Society in Roman Galilee, A.D. 132-212* (Totowa, NJ: Rowman & Allanheld, 1982), pp. 93 ff.

4

prophets, and writings. Since these scriptures were old enough not to be responsive to the most recent social developments, the last few generations of *tannaim* codified subsequent traditions in the form of artificial debates among rabbis ostensibly arguing the esoteric points of scriptural interpretation. This mnemonic device, preserved in the Mishnah, may have encouraged public interest in seemingly arcane points of interpretation by providing a format easily susceptible to memorization in a primarily oral culture. Centuries later, a larger literary *corpus* based on the earlier scriptural and mishnaic *halakah* continues to function as a definitive component of modern Jewish faiths and practices which emphasize the synagogue as the primary religious institution and the written word as the primary basis of authority.

The Jewish canonization and institutionalization process leading to the dissemination of the Mishnah provides an example of especially intentional literary and social developments related closely to each other. The comparable Christian process of the same two centuries seems neither as thorough nor as intentional. Nevertheless, the contemporaneous Christian writings, like their Jewish counterparts, emerged hand-in-glove with institutions. Actually, overt rivalry is a virtual certainty, as the Christian gospels parody the Jewish institutionalization (Jn. 9) and some arcane interests (Matt. 23) of the latter third of the first century; this tendency remains evident at least until the time of Origen. The post-Pauline orthodoxy, which anchors the New Testament with the gospels and the Pauline/deutero-Pauline corpus and treats the other writings as secondary in comparison, informs both the Catholic and the Protestant faiths and practices much as the halakhic tradition continues to inform their Jewish counterparts.

James, in particular, addresses itself openly to ethical concerns, that is, to questions of its audience's cultic, economic, institutional, interpersonal, political, and/or social behavior. In this respect, its presumptive grounding in a group with some standards of accountability renders the epistle comparable to the later, more extensive ethical guidance of the pre-mishnaic traditions. In other words, both the pre-mishnaic traditions and James were written with a view to influencing the development of their audiences' practices. Thus, a rigorous interpretation of the epistle takes as its basis a model of reading which emphasizes the human social impact rather than the mere observation of reality.

The social construction theory of P. Berger and T. Luckmann provides a suitable philosophical underpinning for a reading theory which postulates the influence of formal or informal social accountability upon interpretation.[4] In brief, Berger and Luckmann attribute social cohesion to the linkage of objective with subjective dimensions of reality.[5] The objective aspects include habits, institutions, and legitimations which exist independently of any person. The subjective elements include individual understandings which reinforce the most important of the objective characteristics. Language, the mode of expression of the epistle of James, preserves large amounts of information for considerable periods of time.[6]

Berger and Luckmann, like many of their contemporaries, emphasized the conservative applications of their theory and paid less attention to the possibility that the theory might explain some facets of social development. This possibility received early treatment from K. Mannheim, who noted the social aspects both of ideological, reactionary and of utopian, idealistic thought.[7] More recently in mental health services, proponents of solution-focused therapy have individualized the concept of social construction with an emphasis on personal development. In summary, writing and reading are socially informed activities, with the only question being whether the social dimension is obvious or covert. These activities hold not only the possibility of the social conservatism which Berger and Luckmann emphasized but also that of social development.

Berger and Luckmann's observation that written material serves as a repository of socially conditioned knowledge leads naturally to the use of the sociology of knowledge as a philosophical basis for a model of reading and writing which considers seriously the social dimensions of those activities. The model

---

[4]P. Berger & T. L. Luckmann, *The Social Construction of Reality: A Treatise in the Sociology of Knowledge* (Garden City, NY: Doubleday, 1967).
[5]*Ibid.*, pp. 129-130.
[6]*Ibid.*, p. 37.
[7]*Ideology and Utopia*, tr. L. Wirth & E. Shils (San Diego/New York/London: Harcourt Brace Jovanovich).

postulates a relationship between author and audience and also a process by which control of the written material and of its interpretation passes gradually from the author to the audience. The model is explicitly social and cross-cultural; its specification of the roles of culturally specific criteria and social accountability in the reading process limits the possibility of interpretations absent from any given audience's objective and subjective reality. Owing to its social emphasis, the model probably does not conform to any widely disseminated literary theory. The viability of the model and its five component steps is asserted and explained rather than argued. The accuracy of the model, at least as a guide to conscious reading and publication processes, remains to be determined, but the use of the model in subsequent chapters to provide a rigorous, plausible reading of James constitutes an appropriate test of its utility.

The model begins with the proposition that the relationship between a reader and an author, mediated by a text, includes both adversarial and cooperative characteristics. W. Iser originally suggested that the reader and the text constitute the opposite poles of literary communication.[8] This description becomes more comprehensive when one places the author, rather than the text, at the opposite pole from the reader. The text, then, becomes the medium of communication, the common element with which both the author and the reader must grapple. In the case of extant writings from the first century CE, the words of oral performances and the roles of copyists usually comprised additional layers of communication, potentially enabling the audience to modify the text and to join the author as a co-creator of communication. One cannot ascertain information about these layers readily in the case of James. The oral performances of antiquity, of course, are not available to modern readers for analysis. Furthermore, the Jacobin textual tradition is relatively homogeneous, and the few important textual variants defy solution.[9] Thus, extensive textual criticism (analysis of the roles of copyists as co-creators of the epistle) would provide limited benefit.

---

[8]*The Act of Reading: A Theory of Aesthetic Response* (Baltimore/London: Johns Hopkins Univ., 1978), p. ix.

[9]L. T. Johnson, *The Letter of James* (AB37A; New York/London/Toronto/Sydney/Auckland: Doubleday, 1995), pp. 4-6.

READING JAMES

A text has the potential to elucidate and/or to obscure its own interpretation. This internal polarity may be attributed primarily to the author's techniques. For example, an author may use plain narrative, discourse, logic, and a variety of other techniques to communicate his/her intentions clearly. Likewise, an author may conceal his/her intentions or suggest polyvalent interpretations of a text by using veiled references, circumlocutions, unusual imagery, and figures of speech. James generally uses logical discourse in a concise manner, sometimes with rhetorical flourish. When it creates the possibility of polyvalent interpretation, it does so by means of understatement, to the point of leaving many assumptions implicit. By way of contrast, the Apocalypse emphasizes unusual imagery and figures of speech. The language of most books of the NT falls somewhere between these two extremes owing to the particular qualities inherent in their narrative or epistolary structures.

A reader must respond to the cues which the author places in a text. When an author uses a relatively straightforward style, the reader may follow the cues easily and allow the text to lead him/her to the author's desired conclusion. When the author uses more confusing or polyvalent imagery, the reader must put forth a greater analytical effort to pry a defensible interpretation out of the text. In the first case, the relationship between author and reader is cooperative, with each party to the textual communication working to bring about a desired outcome easily. In the second, the relationship is more adversarial, since the reader must dissect, see through, or resist the author's language in order to produce a coherent or reasonable interpretation. Of course, what constitutes a coherent or reasonable interpretation depends on the standards of the reader and his/her peers, and such standards are highly subjective products of the group's social conditioning.

James and the contrasting Apocalypse require adversarial reading strategies for opposite reasons. The imagery of the Apocalypse is highly symbolic and polyvalent, unless one proposes that the author and a circle of *cognoscenti* shared a highly specialized, in-group language. James, in contrast, exhibits a highly grammatical and rhetorically proficient use of typical Greek vocabulary. Its polyvalence lies in the mundane nature of its contents, the fluidity of its larger divisions, and the implicit character of the author's cultural identity and assumptions. As a result, modern readers (at least) must struggle to interpret James by selecting as their bases of interpretation one or more plausible *Sitze im Leben* from a large number of alternatives. C. Church has summarized the wide variety of proposed generic identifications, historical settings, and interpretations of James resulting from this multiplicity of possible scenarios.[10]

The limits which the author's use of language imposes upon the audience's selection of a reading strategy suggest the model's second proposition. The author sets the ground rules for the game of reading, but the reader has the final word on interpretation. F. Jameson notes that "as texts free themselves more and more from an immediate performance situation, it becomes ever more difficult to enforce a given generic rule on their readers" and identifies the exclusion of undesirable interpretations as an important aspect of the author's writing technique.[11] E. D. Hirsch, Jr. suggests the author's ground rules as the primary factors which identify any given interpretation as valid or invalid.[12] His argument, however, assumes that a reader can identify the author's ground rules and use them to exlude undesirable interpretations. The uncertainty surrounding both the identity of the author of James and the *Sitze im Leben* of the earliest audiences demonstrates not only the relevance of Jameson's warning but also the lack of sufficient data to use Hirsch's otherwise worthwhile criterion in the analysis of James.

The dissemination of a text entails the author's surrender of control over interpretation. In some cases, such as the publication of *Huckleberry Finn*, this process may include the author's modification of a manuscript to cater to audience preferences.[13] As a text enters the public domain, any reader is free to perform his own analysis and to draw his own conclusions. A living author's opportunity to interpret his own published text is roughly equivalent to any other reader's opportunity to interpret the same text; for example, R. Crosman cites E. Pound's

---

[10]*A Forschungsgeschichte on the Literary Character of the Epistle of James.* (Louisville, KY: Unpublished Ph.D. diss., Southern Baptist Theological Seminary, 1990).

[11]*The Political Unconscious: Narrative as a Socially Symbolic Act* (Ithaca, NY: Cornell Univ.), pp. 106-107.

[12]*Validity in Interpretation* (New York/London: Yale Univ., 1967), p. 200.

[13]G. Condon, "The Return of Huckleberry Finn," Louisville *Courier-Journal, Sat.*, 4/20/96, A15.

9

suggestion in 1916 of three possible interpretations of a short poem which Pound had written in 1914.[14] The limitations on interpretation include the author's intention only when it is known and when the reader is a constituent of a community which values authorial intention as a criterion for interpretation.

The success with which an author communicates his/her intended degree of clarity depends substantially on the acculturation of the reader. A shared language, culture, perspective, and series of literary conventions increase the probability of close correspondence between authorial intention and reader response. The lack of common elements, conversely, increases the probability of discrepancy between authorial intention and reader response. Since this latter condition characterizes the relationship between modern, western audiences and the author of James, the construction of hypothetical but plausible first century audiences increases the probability of a twentieth century interpretation which accounts for the conditions of the epistle's provenance in classical antiquity.

The influence of the reader's community on the standards of acceptable interpretation suggests the third proposition of the reading model. Whether reading is verbal and communal, the norm during classical antiquity,[15] or silent and individual, the interpretation process is a social endeavor. A reader draws conclusions in light of his/her community's body of common knowledge and standard practices. J. Leenhardt's comparison of the reading strategies used by a French and a Hungarian group for the same novels, one from each country, indicates that both groups interpreted the foreign novel in light of their own "national patterns of literary perception" and "unifying cultural schemes."[16] In the case of writings to which religious groups accord prominence, the standards of interpretation may transcend national and linguistic distinctions. A common culture informed the mindset of readers throughout the Mediterranean basin during the

---

[14]"Do Readers Make Meaning?" In S. R. Suleiman & I. Crosman, eds., *The Reader in the Text: Essays on Audience and Interpretation* (Princeton, NJ: Princeton Univ., 1980), pp. 149-164.

[15]P. Achtemeier, *Omne Verbum Sonat: The New Testament and the Oral Environment of Late Western Antiquity," Journal of Biblical Literature*, 109/1 (1990), 3-27.

[16]"Towards a Sociology of Reading," tr. B. Navelet & S. R. Suleiman, in *The Reader in the Text*, p. 223, c.f., pp. 214-219.

Hellenistic and the Roman eras.[17] Even today, fundamentalist, liberal, neo-orthodox, skeptical and other approaches to scripture, and the religious and social practices which follow logically from these approaches, are equally evident in Judaism, Christianity, and Islam, the three major religions which originated in the ancient Mediterranean basin and persist in numerous, modern settings.

Whenever a particular reader's conclusions depart markedly from the accepted standards, either of the following processes of reconciliation may ensue: (1) The community suppresses the reader's unusual interpretation or convinces the reader to conform to accepted standards, or (2) The community accepts the new interpretation or a portion thereof and incorporates it into a new *status quo*. Such reconciliation processes and the resulting compromises are proposed in some of the mishnaic debates and, among early Christian writings, in Acts 15 and Gal. 2.

The didactic method which D. Bleich uses in his English literature classes illustrates the influence of social factors on interpretation. Bleich defends the primacy of subjective elements in interpretation and uses social control rather than his individual authority to limit the extent of controversial readings among his students. He bases his method on J. Piaget's theory regarding social control over the development of intelligence and reasoning ability:

> The social group ... plays the same role that the "population" does in genetics and consequently in instinct. In this sense, society is the supreme unit, and the individual can only achieve his own inventions and intellectual constructions insofar as he is the seat of collective interactions that are naturally dependent, in level and value, on society as a whole.[18]

Bleich's process begins, of course, with readings of the assigned works. Response statements from the students constitute the next step in the process, and

---

[17]This is the major point of M. Hengel's influential survey, *Judaism and Hellenism: Studies in Their Encounter in Palestine During the Early Hellenistic Period*, tr. J. Bowden (London: SCM/Philadelphia: Fortress, 1974), 2 vols., *passim*.

[18]J. Piaget, *Biology and Knowledge*, tr. B. Walsh (Edinburgh: Edinburgh Univ., 1971), p. 369, as quoted in D. Bleich, *Subjective Criticism* (Baltimore/London: Johns Hopkins Univ., 1978), p. 29.

the needs of the class as a whole subsequently determine the negotiability of the response statements.[19] This process results in the development of accepted interpretations, possibly amenable to characterization as authoritative for the purposes of the class, by means of consensus. "Determining the negotiability of response statements is part of the communal definition of its purposes and part of the delineation of individual responsiblity within the group."[20] The revision of individual students' responses to particular works, in light of social influences, is inherent in the learning process. The effect of encouragement to analyze authorial background and intention on one student's response to a work by W. Joyce illustrates both the social aspects of interpretation and the reader's responsibility for the use of any criteria, including authorial intention and original setting.[21]

The majority of the examples in Bleich's book convey the impression that Bleich encourages his students to emphasize the individual, psychological ramifications of their reading strategies. This orientation is not normally associated with the academic analysis of ancient texts, an observation which supports the hypothesis of social control over interpretation in the case of the academic interpreters. Academic analysis, though, like the reader response by Bleich's students, occurs in accordance with a socially defined paradigm. In an analogous manner, social pressures influenced the development of texts of interest to scholars of several religious traditions. Both the Christian canonization process and the Qumran community's deviant interpretation of well-known Jewish texts during the composition of its own literary corpus may be understood as conscious, explicit social efforts to determine the limits of the respective religious communities' acceptable interpretations of their writings. The gradual development of the halakhic literature within mainstream Judaism may be viewed as an especially long-lived and highly focused example of the development of a written corpus and a socially defined paradigm in close connection with each other.

The social influence on the development of guidelines for writing and reading leads to the fourth proposition of the reading model. Interpretation

---

[19]Bleich, *Subjective Criticism*, pp. 188-189.

[20]Bleich, *Subjective Criticism*, p. 189.

[21]*Ibid.*, pp. 238-263.

depends largely on socially approved classification schemata. As described above, an author may or may not propose clear literary conventions to guide readers in the selection of appropriate criteria for interpretation.[22] Regardless of how an author handles this matter, the reader, influenced by his/her social norms and peers, makes the final selection. The choice of heuristic criteria constitutes a *de facto* classification of the work; to paraphrase G. Linton, the construction of a generic identity allows a reader to interpret a text in terms of its similarities with selected other texts.[23] Thus, genre is a social as well as a literary concept. The mutual influence of interpretation and conditions within a reader's group of peers suggest that genre may be defined as the comparison of written works on the basis of socially validated criteria.

In a relatively clear situation, Jameson's forensic, metaphorical description of genre summarizes the social dimensions of the literary enterprise. According to this description, "genres are essentially literary *institutions,* or social contracts between a writer and a specified public, whose function is to specify the proper use of a particular cultural artifact.[24] To extend the metaphor in a different direction, however, the analogy of a social contract may be fraught with difficulties when a work lacks clear indications of literary convention or is read by a public which differs markedly from the one specified. Such difficulties are particularly salient in the cases of ancient texts, the authors and earliest audiences of which have been deceased for several centuries. Jameson's description of genre assumes that the actual reader is similar in key respects to some plausible target.

The interpretation of a text depends partially on the reader's decision regarding its genre, that is, the reader's selection of other works as objects of comparison. The author's intentions regarding genre and interpretation are important data which should inform the reader's interpretive method; this is the major point of Hirsch's influential work. However, in the absence of especially clear criteria, whatever is known of the author's intention is likely to provide no

---

[22] For a fuller discussion in terms of a particular NT text, see G. Linton, "Reading the Apocalypse as an Apocalypse," *SBL Seminar Papers*, 30 (1991), 161-186.
[23] Ibid., pp. 161, 166-167.
[24] *The Political Unconscious*, p. 106, emphasis in the original.

more than an indication of which possible genre are defensible and which are indefensible, this very situation facilitates the numerous and sometimes polyvalent readings of James. A reader is responsible for his/her interpretation of any given text and must acknowledge the influence both of his/her own background and social location and of the available data about the author on that interpretation.

The fifth proposition of the reading model states that a reader's generic assumptions regarding a particular text may be arranged hierarchically. To push T. L. Kent's journalistic example[25] in a different direction, the following generic identifications, ranging from the most widely to the most narrowly focused, would be defensible for an editorial cartoon: a given number of newspaper column inches; a line drawing; a cartoon; an editorial cartoon; a statement of opinion; an interpretation of newsworthy events, institutions, or persons; and an interpretation of the newsworthy in the form of political satire, household hints, policy advocacy, or some other such category. Each of these characterizations would meet the test of pragmatism, but each would push the reader towards a different basis of comparison and thus towards a different perspective from which to interpret the editorial cartoon.

The variety of plausible generic classifications for any given text suggests that one may characterize genre in a manner analogous to taxonomy in the natural sciences. This observation suggests a cautionary note for a reader's formulation of generic assumptions. Animals are classified into kingdoms, phyla, classes, orders, families, genera, and species, with each grouping narrower than its predecessor. The nature of each grouping is determined by the number of types of organisms and the extent of the differences among organisms which the grouping includes and thus defines as similar on some level. An organism belongs to a kingdom, phylum, class, order, family, genus, and species simultaneously because zoologists have devised their taxonomy to function hierarchically. Due to this intentionally hierarchical structure, an analytical tool rather than an intrinsic characteristic of the organisms under observation, a zoologist is likely to derive the most coherent

---

[25]*Interpretation and Genre: The Role of Generic Perception in the Study of Narrative Texts* (Lewisburg, PA: Bucknell Univ., 1986), pp. 16-19.

conclusions by studying an organism only in terms of one level of comparison at a time. In the event that one must interpret smaller, self-contained units within a text diachronically, D. Hellholm's concept of "conceptual hierarchicalization" provides a caveat to limit both uncritical importation of taxonomy from the natural to the social sciences and reliance on hierarchical generic classifications.[26]

One may summarize this social model of the reading process by comparing reading to the production of a physical artifact. Ancient texts, including James, serve as raw materials for the intellectual constructions of modern readers. Other relevant data, when available, also serve as raw materials for intellectual constructions. Such data may include awareness of authorial circumstances and intentions, specific circumstances of early audiences, general cultural conditions in which the texts were disseminated, and the modern reader's own cultural, social, and intellectual heritage. Readers choose from the available raw materials, use them in various combinations, and perform the ensuing intellectual operations. Social accountability processes, such as external refereeing and editing, and the interpreter's internal limitations, such as theoretical constructs, serve functions analogous to those of various guidelines, procedures, and regulations by limiting the extent of the possibly hazardous or irrelevant intellectual constructs. Thus, the modern reader of James has an opportunity to use the tools of intellectual activity to produce an interpretation consistent both with what can be known of the situations surrounding its earliest dissemination and with the requirements of twentieth century readers, within the limits imposed by the scarcity of data regarding many facets of the epistle's composition and early dissemination.

Social Characteristics of Modern Readings of James

The social model of reading, described above, provides an apt heuristic framework for the summary evaluation of modern readings of James. The treatments of James by academic interpreters of the past century demonstrate the

---

[26]"The Problem of Apocalyptic Genre and the Apocalypse of John," *Semeia: An Experimental Journal for Biblical Criticism*, 36 (1986), 13-64.

hallmarks of attempts to bridge the cultural and temporal chasm between the work in its initial and modern settings, peer accountability on the part of the writers, and socially defined classification schemata amenable to hierarchical arrangement. The following pages provide a brief summary of the treatments of the epistle's authorship in three substantial contributions to scholarship from the turn of the century. The topics are analyzed in terms of the heuristic framework described above and also provide illustrative material of a limited nature. The commentaries by Mayor, Ropes, and Dibelius lay a foundation for much of the subsequent analysis of James.[27] C. Church and the introductions to most substantial commentaries provide several extensive descriptions of the past century's research relevant to the epistle.[28]

The social model of reading begins with the proposition that the text under consideration constitutes the medium for a relationship between author and reader. Furthermore, this relationship includes both adversarial and cooperative aspects. All three commentators acknowledged this proposition by developing and asserting their assumptions or conclusions regarding the author's identity and the nature of the text before they produced their own interpretations of the text. In short, the commentators considered the identificaton of their theoretical partner in the communication process a major delineator of the interpretation of the literary artifact for which this ancient author was responsible.

The question of authorship epitomizes the simultaneously adversarial and cooperative character of the text of James. The epistolary praescript (1:1) provides the author's given name. However, the name Ἰάκωβος tells us little about the author's affiliations, identity, interests, and world-view. If one should examine any city's residential phone directory, find a common surname (e.g., Miller, Smith, Williams), cover the surname column, and then count the entries for persons named Giacomo, Jacob, Jaime Jake, Jay, Jamie, James, Jim, and Jimmy, he would gain an impression of the extent to which the given name by itself provides

---

[27]J. B. Mayor, *Epistle of James*, loc. cit. J. H. Ropes, *A Critical and Exegetical Commentary on the Epistle of St. James* (ICC; Edinburgh: T. & T. Clark, 1916). M. Dibelius, *Der Brief des Jakobus* (KEKNT; Göttingen: Vandenhoeck & Ruprecht, 1921).

[28]*Forschungsgeschichte on the Literary Character*, loc. cit. on p. 9 above.

usable information about an otherwise unidentified author. Owing to the small selection and frequent duplication of personal names in many ancient societies, some groups, such as those in which the first and third gospels circulated, used genealogies to identify individuals more clearly. The author of the epistle, in contrast, provided only his given name, a decision which creates a level of uncertainty for modern audiences, though not necessarily for the earliest ones.

All three commentators decided whether or not to fill in the blanks regarding the author's identity. Mayor began his work with a lengthy chapter defending the traditional attribution of the epistle to Jesus' brother James.[29] Ropes, in contrast, satisfied himself with a brief treatment, concluding only that the epistle was written in Palestine sometime before 150 CE by someone named James; he expressed sympathy for though not willingness to commit to the position of pseudonymous authorship by an otherwise anonymous Palestinian teacher, with the epistolary praescript intended to evoke the authority of Jesus' brother.[30] Dibelius' treatment of the authorship question represents a middle ground, regarding detail and length, between those of the two English-language authors. Dibelius concluded that the author's facility with literate Greek, apparent awareness of some aspects of the Pauline concepts of faith and works, and unfamiliarity with Jewish ritual practices militated against attribution to Jesus' brother; on this basis, he mounted a strong defense of the theory of pseudonymity.[31] Of course, he based this assessment on the stereotype of Jesus' brother as a hide-bound traditionalist and the assumption that he participated only peripherally in the Pauline debates regarding the standards of Christian identity.[32]

If one could attribute the epistle to Jesus' brother James with any degree of certainty, he could avail himself of the tradition regarding this person to elucidate the circumstances to which, and possibly also the persons to whom, the author addressed the text. Generally, the more conservative commentators follow Mayor's lead in attributing the text to Jesus' brother and supplying an eastern

---

[29] *Epistle of James*, pp. i-xlvii.
[30] *Critical and Exegetical Commentary*, pp. 48-52.
[31] *Der Brief des Jakobus*, pp. 11-19.
[32] *Ibid.*, pp. 11-15.

Mediterranean (frequently Palestinian) *Sitz im Leben* for the earliest audiences.[33] Thus, a firm assumption regarding authorship enables conservative commentators to bring a set of assumptions regarding early Christian history to bear on the text. More sanguine interpreters, following the lead of Ropes or Dibelius, lack the foundation which the conservatives obtain from the traditional attribution.[34] Such interpreters formulate plausible backgrounds for the epistle on the basis of cultural and historical assumptions which are informative in general terms but may not provide information as specific to the case at hand as would the identification of a definite author and/or his intended audience. Consequently, the conservative perspective provides an advantageous position from which to state assumptions regarding the background of the text, but the sanguine position remains more consistent with the uncertainty of the material basis of the assumptions.

The equivocal nature of the evidence regarding the authorship of the epistle brings into play the second proposition of the social model of reading. The author sets the ground rules for reading, but the reader has the final say regarding interpretation. As described above, the three commentaries on James analyzed one self-designation by one author in one brief work in one literary context. Thus, the author, by providing only partial information regarding his identity, imposed limits with which all three modern commentators grappled. Mayor addressed this gap by recourse to the traditional attribution of authorship, the requisite early date (50's CE), and acceptance of the epistolary framework as the letter's primary organizing principal.[35] Ropes, in contrast with Mayor, supplied a *Sitz im Leben* characterized by a post-apostolic stage of institutional development, unfamiliarity with the major issues pervading post-Pauline Christianity, and limited exposure to Hellenistic moral teachings.[36] He emphasized the verbal aspects of the early readings of the letter, classifying its style as the Hellenistic diatribe.[37] Dibelius, adding detail to

---

[33]See, for example, P. H. Davids, *The Epistle of James: A Commentary on the Greek Text* (NIGCT; Grand Rapids: William B. Eerdmans, 1982), pp. 2-13, 28-34.

[34]Davids notes this difference repeatedly (e.g., *Epistle of James*, p. 28).

[35]*Epistle of James*, pp. cxxi-cxxiv.

[36]*Critical and Exegetical Commentary*, pp. 48-49.

[37]*Ibid.*, pp. 10-16.

Ropes' proposals in a number of respects, proposed a scenario in which the author was aware of the Pauline faith-works dichotomy but not familiar with its nuances. Ropes' implied author communicated his ethical teaching in the form of a loosely organized *paraenesis*, or collection of brief, general admonitions connected only by the repetition of key words from one precept in the following statement.[38]

The three proposals regarding authorship and circumstances of composition illustrate the reader's responsibility for interpretation, even when all readers operate within the identical limit imposed by the author's text. The format which the three academic writers selected illustrates the third proposition of the social model of reading, that, interpretation is a social endeavor. The commentary format, then, as now, received wide acceptance as an appropriate vehicle for substantial academic publication in certain disciplines. This scholarly convention becomes evident as the reader compares the outlines of the three works. All three begin with long introductions describing the author's assumptions or conclusions regarding authorship, date, provenance, historical setting, and relationship to other canonical and non-canonical writings, with some variation in the order of topics. The commentaries continue with verse-by-verse explanations of the epistle in propositional format; this central section occupies the bulk of the pages. Finally, all three conclude with extensive indices to guide the reader in the topical examination of the commentaries. This basic format may be found in many other commentaries from the past several centuries, not only in those on James but also in those covering virtually every canonical and related work. The choice of the commentary format by all three authors corroborates the indication which the pervasive character of the commentary format provides. All three authors followed the conventions of their peer group, the academic community, in their interpretations of James. They selected the format, language, and accessories which defined a substantial, rigorous publication of large scale in the traditions of their chosen discipline.

The academic community shared common conventions regarding the commentary format, and these conventions extended across national boundaries.

---

[38] *Der Brief des Jakobus*, pp. 1-10.

However, one should avoid characterizing the academic community as a monolith. Then, as now, the academic community included representatives of divinity schools, seminaries, and university religious studies departments. Some received their salaries from the state, others from the church, and still others from private, non-sectarian sources. The contributions of Darwin in the natural sciences set the stage for conservative vs. liberal controversies, particularly in the English-speaking nations. The American emphasis on applied and the German emphasis on theoretical formulations colored the contributions of scholars from those nations in the humanities as well as the natural and social sciences. In the case of the three works discussed here, the British commentary (Mayor) seems to be the most conservative, coming from a society in which the academic community and the established church catered to the same socioeconomic elite. The American commentary (Ropes) occupies a middle ground regarding most critical questions. Finally, the German contribution (Dibelius) models a diachronic approach on the form critical work which the same author, one of his students (Schmidt), and one of his peers (Bultmann) had pioneered independently of each other only a few years earlier, in their 1918 and 1919 publications on the synoptic gospels.

All three commentators based their assumptions or conclusions regarding authorship on the characteristics of the epistle which they defined as most salient. These predilections arose in accordance with the social validation provided by the characteristics of their subdivisions of the academic community. In other words, the importance of socially validated comparison, the fourth proposition of the social model of reading, becomes evident in the bases for the commentator's conclusions regarding authorship. Dibelius emphasized the brevity of and loose connections among the segments of the epistle and argued that hellenistic philosophical treatises constituted the most suitable basis of comparison.[39] His assumption regarding authorship proceeded largely from this conclusion regarding the salient characteristics of the epistle. In a culture which emphasized classical education and exposure to primary sources in Greek and Latin, Dibelius' choice of comparative material proceeded naturally from the orientation which Dibelius' and

---

[39] Der *Brief des Jakobus*, pp. 1-10.

his peers' academic training provided and received validation from the academic peers with comparable training and orientations..

On the opposite end of the spectrum, Mayor's conservative assumption regarding authorship arose from his emphasis on the unity provided by the letter's ostensible epistolary character. This position carried with it the reasonable expectation of validation by Mayor's peers in England's elitist academic environment. In addition, the position presumed the use of other early Christian epistles, rather than philosophical treatises, as objects of comparison, another characteristic which conservative audiences might find congenial. Ropes' cautious defense of pseudonymous authorship, based on the oral (diatribe) style of the letter, constituted a middle ground calculated to receive validation in an American culture of higher education. In this setting, neither the elitist orientation nor the exposure to Greek and Latin primary sources was as highly developed as they were in the older educational traditions of the European nations.

The fifth proposition of the social model of reading asserts that an analyst may arrange generic assumptions hierarchically. The selection of comparative material discussed above illustrates this point. Each author identified one characteristic of the epistle, rather than any other characteristic, as most important in the definition of the interpretive task. Each author, of course, chose a different characteristic. Mayor selected the epistolary form, Ropes the oral qualities, and Dibelius the brief sayings with loose connections. Consequently, the three authors steered their interpretations in three different directions.

The use of these commentaries by successive commentators illustrates both the fourth and the fifth propositions of the model. Each of the three perspectives received validation in the form of publication and wide circulation, of course. More recent commentators have tried to synthesize the three perspectives into more unified theories. The conservative attempt by Davids illustrates the hierarchical arrangement of these generic assumptions inherent in most syntheses. Davids proposed a two-stage theory of composition. He suggested that a subsequent redactor compiled sermons and sayings originating with Jesus' brother

James for public reading as a circular epistle.[40] This synthesis implies that the generic assumptions regarding the epistle may be arranged from widest to narrowest scope of comparison as follows: Epistle, letter written in a rhetorical style suited to public performance, and edited compilation of sayings. At this point, one should note that Davids' proposal of the synagogue homily rather than the diatribe as a description of the middle level of comparison reflects the post-WWII increase in interest in the Jewish aspects of Christian origins.[41]   F. Mussner's redactional study, like that of Davids, proposes a compilation of sayings in a homily style similar to the diatribe. However, Mussner contrasts the epistle's synthesis of faith and works with Paul's polemic approach and concludes, in contrast to Davids, that the epistle presumes some consideration and assimilation of the Pauline position and its opposite.[42]

The Polyvalent Context of James

The social model of reading provides a heuristic framework for the analysis of interpretation. The development of meaning or usage usually occurs rapidly and without the step-by-step reasoning which the model might imply. In addition, the model grows primarily from twentieth century concepts of intellectual development, literature, and social psychology. The application of the model to three modern commentators' considerations of the identity of the author of James demonstrates, however, that the model can be applied informatively to academically rigorous works predicated explicitly on other concerns. Whether or not the model is useful for the analysis of ancient literature remains open to question. An initial experiment indicated that the model may guide the reader in an examination of the literary and social assumptions which some first century audiences may have brought to another NT work.[43] The brief inquiry below

---

[40]*Epistle of James*, pp. 12-13, 21-22.

[41]*Ibid.*, p. 23.

[42]*Der Jakobusbrief* (HTKNT; Freiburg/Basel/Wein: Herder, 1964), pp. 12-21.

[43]R. C. Webber, "The Apocalypse as Utopia: Ancient and Modern Subjectivity," *SBL Seminar Papers*, 32 (1993), 104-118.

describes the disparate interpretations of James' treatment of Abraham which are plausible for various possible first century audiences.

The treatment of Abraham constitutes the central section of the epistle. This discussion seems to form an intellectual fulcrum on which many of the preceeding and subsequent arguments turn. In 2:14-26, James urged his audience to follow the example of Abraham, for whom works accompanied and completed faith. He cited Abraham's offering of Isaac as a sacrifice to prove his point (2:21-22) but then summarized with a direct quotation of Gen. 15:6 (LXX), the same verse and translation that Paul quoted directly in Gal. 3:6 and Rom. 4:3 to buttress his argument that Christians, like Abraham, their forbear, were justified by faith rather than by works.

The similarities of James' and Paul's arguments might encourage a post-Pauline Christian to assume that the later author tried to contradict or correct the earlier. Some commentators have reached this conclusion rather quickly. M. Hengel, for example, argues the position forcefully, developing the hypothesis that James launched a direct attack against both the pragmatic and the theological aspects of Paul's missionary practices.[44] The commentator who adopts this perspective, of course, makes five assumptions. First, Paul preceded James chronologically. Second, Paul's treatment of Abraham in Gal. 3 and Rom. 4 already had become normative among some Greek-speaking Christians by the time James wrote his epistle. Third, the author of James counted his audiences among those who considered the Pauline formulation regarding faith and works normative. Fourth, the Pauline and the Jacobin formulations represent the opposite extremes of an ideological spectrum concerning the topic of Abraham. Fifth, the Pauline formulation constitutes the only suitable background for its Jacobin counterpart.

---

[44]"Der Jakobusbrief als antipaulinische Polemik," in *Tradition and Interpretation in the New Testament: Essays in Honor of E. Earle Ellis for His Sixtieth Birthday*, ed. G. F. Hawthorne & O. Betz (Grand Rapids, MI/Tübingen: William B. Eerdmans/J. C. B. Mohr [Paul Siebeck], 1987), p. 265. Cf., C. E. Donker, "Der Verfasser des Jakobus und sein Gegner: Zum Problem des Einwandes in Jak. 2:18-19," *Zeitschrift für die Neutestamentliche Wissenschaft und die Kunde der Älteren Kirche*, 72 (1981), 237-242.

Actually, all of the conditions described above are assumptions rather than certainties. The most certain aspect of the background is the language, that is, the aspect which is both available to twentieth century audiences and amenable to comparison. This aspect is tangential to the assumptions above. The author or his amanuensis showed no reluctance to display his facility with a fairly literate grade of Greek, complete with rhetorical flourishes. This facility included the frequent use of the LXX in the epistle, so the author most likely used the version due to familiarity rather than simply to defeat Paul at his own game. Regarding the assumption of a late date for James, the author's or amanuensis' proficiency in Greek alone may militate against but is insufficient to rule out the early date and Palestinian provenance which the conservative commentators prefer.[45] The first three assumptions above are subject to debate. The last two clearly are invalid. The discussion below demonstrates that the Jacobin and the Pauline formulations do not constitute opposite poles and that there is a wide range of comparative material relevant to the use of Abraham as an example during the period.

Each assumption becomes defensible when the commentator defines a hypothetical, first century audience in accordance with the assumption. In other words, each commentator's assumptions regarding the relationship of James to Paul depend heavily on the commentator's description of an implied reader. For example, Hengel's late first century audience is familiar with the Pauline formulation; consequently, Hengel presents James as an example of anti-Pauline polemic.[46] Davids, in contrast, with his early date and Palestinian provenance, proposes an audience relatively unfamiliar with Pauline thought. Consequently, he concludes that James addressed this section to mainstream Jewish faith and practice rather than to the Pauline formulation.[47] In this respect, his description of the audience and composition of James has the practical effect of conforming the

---

[45]See S. Laws, *The Epistle of James* (BNTC; Peabody, MA: Hendrickson, 1980), p. 40 and Davids, *Epistle of James*, pp. 10-13. In addition, Acts 6:1-7 describes a bilingual scenario which one first-century author found plausible for Jerusalem, and Goodman (*State and Society in Roman Galilee*, pp. 66-68) argues that residents of Galilee spoke Greek to some extent.

[46]"Der Jakobusbrief als antipaulinische Polemik," pp. 258-262.

[47]*Epistle of James*, p. 125.

position of James regarding Abraham to that of Paul. Both Hengel's and Davids' arguments, like many others, are circular in character. The analyst uses information derived from the text to construct a hypothetical audience and then uses the hypothetical audience as the basis for the assumptions which guide his interpretation of the text.

The first three assumptions are subject to debate, with circular reasoning prevalent in the consideration of the relevant issues. One may bring evidence external to James and the Pauline corpus to bear on the fourth and fifth assumptions, however. One may construct a hypothetical spectrum of first and second century opinions of Abraham by recourse to literature other than James and the Pauline corpus and then may place both authors' contributions in their larger context. Given the chronological range of the materials, one cannot conclude that this larger context defined the intellectual milieu of the earliest audiences of James. The epistle antedates several of the other examples, and, in any case, the aspects of this range of tradition, if any, which the author and earliest audiences may have found familiar are uncertain. Thus, the context proves informative but not conclusive for the development of a hypothesis regarding either the author's or the audience's assumptions and characteristics. On the other hand, the possible influence of the Jacobin and the Pauline formulations on the development of the subsequent *tannaitic* traditions about Abraham might constitute a fruitful topic of investigation. This approach, though beyond the scope of the current inquiry, is consistent with the relative chronological positions of the NT and the rabbinic writings.

We begin our consideration of the tradition regarding Abraham as an example of faith and/or works with writings by Philo of Alexandria (c. 20-50 CE), a contemporary of Paul's. This author is notable for the volume and variety of his comments on Abraham. His predilection for allegorical interpretation distinguishes his use of the Abraham traditions from the use to which the Christian and later *tannaitic* writers discussed below put the same traditions. Due to the variety of his perspectives on Abraham, one finds it difficult to pin down Philo's precise thought regarding the relationship between faith and works, as exemplified by Abraham. More importantly, however, Philo uses the same scripture passages to debate the same questions to which Paul, James, other NT authors, and subsequent Jewish writers devoted considerable attention.

For sheer quantity, Philo's citation of Gen. 15:6 surpasses the use to which other writers put the same passage. In *Leg. All.* 3:228, he cited the verse to encourage a belief in God which he characterized in rational terms. Like the later redactors of the Mekilta, he continued with the example of Moses after his discussion of Abraham. In this passage, he did not address himself to works of any sort or to Torah observance explicitly. In *Q. De. Immut. Sit* 3-4, he paraphrased the verse at the conclusion of a passage in which Abraham's demonstration of his faith by sacrificing Isaac formed a point of departure for Philo's interpretation. In this case, the point of departure was quite similar to the reasoning of Heb. 11 and the example in Jas. 2. *Q. Re. Div. Heres* 90-93 cited Abraham's belief in God as an example of the assent to the concept of a single deity which Philo proposes; in this respect, Philo's orientation bears an ironic similarity to the sarcastic remark which enables James to bring suitable emphasis to his point in 2:19.

Philo departed from his typically vague style at the conclusion of one of his two books about Abraham. In *De. Abr.* 273-276, he paraphrased Gen. 15:6 to praise Abraham's faith and continued with a citation of Gen. 26:5, to demonstrate that Abraham observed the law and commandments before they were given to his descendents in written form. This passage may elaborate upon the suggestion which Jesus b. Sirach made in Ecclus. 44:20, a work translated into Greek in Alexandria a couple of centuries before Philo. Finally, *De Virt.* 214-216 summarizes Gen. 15:6 in connection with Abraham's departure from his homeland, a connection which the author of Hebrews also would make a few years later. In this work, as in *Q. De. Immut. Sit*, Philo's proposed correlation of faith and works both was tangential to the topic of Torah observance and served as a point of departure for subsequent interpretation.

Philo devoted two entire books to the topic of Abraham. *De Migratione Abrahami* opens with a citation of Gen. 12:1 and departs into an allegorical consideration of the dualistic aspects of human nature. *De Abrahamo* interprets Abraham's departure from Harran as the concrete action which served as both a springboard and an allegory for Abraham's renunciation of astrology and Chaldean polytheism. This mildly allegorical interpretation sets the stage for Philo's conclusion, on the basis of Gen. 26:5, that Abraham observed the law long before it was promulgated in its oral and written form.

Several of the NT writings, aside from those of Paul and James, include traditions regarding Abraham, but only one, Heb. 11, includes an explicit discussion of the relationship of Abraham's faith to his works. This passage characterizes Abraham's departure from Haran to an unknown inheritance, subsequent migrations, power of procreation, and sacrifice of Isaac as behaviors resulting naturally from his faith (Heb. 11:8-19). Thus, the author of Hebrews assumes a position regarding the faith-works dichotomy which incorporates aspects of both the Jacobin and the Pauline emphases. The subsidiary example of Rahab (Heb. 11:31, Jas. 2:25) is sufficient to illustrate both the similarities and the differences between Hebrews and James in this respect. One work attributes her hospitality towards the Israelite spies (a readily available, written tradition about a specific incident) to faith and the other to works. As noted above, Hebrews develops some of the same Abraham traditions to which Philo attended but limits its dualism to a less thorough form than that which Philo proposed.

The scope of the Mishnaic traditions about Abraham is comparable to the variety seen in Philo and the NT. An anonymous tradition in M.Ab. 5:19 identifies a good eye, humble spirit, and lowly soul as the three characteristics of the "disciples of Abraham" and their opposites as the stereotypical features of the "disciples of Balaam the wicked." This tradition apparently emphasizes works in a sense other than that of works of the law and thereby deemphasizes the connection between Abraham and Torah observance. M.Ab. 5:3, which asserts Abraham's steadfast resistance to ten temptations, exhibits the same emphasis. A statement attributed to R. Nehorai (c. 165-200 CE), in contrast, interprets Gen. 26:5 as an assertion that Abraham observed the Torah in its entirety before its promulgation (M.Kidd. 4:14). This interpretaton is virtually identical to that which Philo reached at the end of *De Abr.* on the basis of the same verse of Genesis. Nehorai's interpretation contradicts that attributed to the slightly earlier R. Ishmael b. Elisha (c. 120-140 CE). The successors of this rabbi, himself an important contributor to the pre-Mishnaic traditions, cited Gen. 15:6 in a roughly contemporaneous work to assert that "our father Abraham inherited both this world and the world beyond only as a reward for the faith with which he believed..." (Mek.Bes. 7:141). This assertion subsequently became the lynchpin for a major theme of the Mekilta, that the Israelites were redeemed from Egypt "only as a reward for the faith with which they believed" (Mek. Bes. 7:142-144). Ishmael's position and use of the Hebrew scriptures seem quite compatible with Paul's, though Ishmael's situation apparently was less polarized than those to which Paul addressed Galatians and Romans.

The summary above brings into sharp relief a spectrum of opinion regarding the relationship of Abraham's faith to his works. On the right side stand Philo (*De Abr.*) and Nehorai, one a Hellenized contemporary of Paul and the other a later Galilean *tanna* whose traditions were preserved in Hebrew. They used Gen. 26:5 to defend the proposition that Abraham was an observant Jew, even though the Torah was promulgated long after his death. On the left stand Paul, an early writer who used Greek, and Ishmael, a *tanna* whose successors redacted his interpretation of Exodus in Hebrew. Both argued, on the basis of a very literalistic interpretation of Gen. 15:6, that Abraham and his successors were justified by faith apart from works of the law. Other comments by Philo, the traditions in M.Ab., Heb. 11, and James 2 illustrate a variety of mediating and synthesizing positions. In summary, all of the writers whose works are described above had recourse to the same traditions preserved in the same scriptures, with only minor differences among the recensions. Each author, informed by his intellectual heritage, agenda, and possibility of audience validation, assumed responsibility for the way in which he incorporated the Abraham tradition into his own work. Consequently, one set of Abraham traditions serves as a point of departure for several contrasting first and second century CE elaborations.

Among Christian and Jewish writers of the first two centuries CE, the full range of the Abraham tradition is evident across the barriers of culture, language, and time. Thus, one may sustain the proposition that the full range of the tradition most likely had undergone its initial development by the time James was written. Philo wrote during the Caligula regime, and Paul was either earlier than or contemporaneous with James. Furthermore, the interpretation of Gen. 15:6, and, to a lesser extent, that of Gen. 26:5, played pivotal roles in the development of the tradition. It is impossible, however, to determine the extent to which either the author or the earliest audiences of James were aware of this range of tradition. In other words, the spectrum described above is an heuristic model constructed to benefit the analytical purposes of twentieth century readers rather than a precise reflection of any specific ancient audience's use of the Abraham traditions.

The position of James as a moderate within the entire scope of the tradition is evident but must be stated in comparative rather than in absolute terms. James is moderate in comparison with Paul and Ishmael on the one hand and with Nehorai and Philo (*De Abr.*) on the other. This obvious conclusion, however, does not imply that James intended to mediate between a Philonic and a Pauline position or that his audiences would have interpreted his letter in such a matter. We simply do not know what James intended or whether he and his audiences compared his position to the entire range of the tradition or simply to some components thereof. Thus, at least theoretically, James 2 is explicable as a response to Gal. 3 and Rom 4, or, for those who assign to James an early date, vice versa. However, James has no intrinsic characteristics necessitating the hypothesis of a response to the Pauline formulation. Conversely, Paul's vituperative remarks in Galatians do no more than suggest the opposite possibility, assuming that one is willing to associate the epistle of James with Jesus' brother and then to assign the epistle's position regarding Abraham to Jesus' brother at an early stage in his relationship to Paul.

The consideration of James' interpretation of Abraham brings us to the very point which we reached with the social model of reading and again with the consideration of some academic commentators' treatments of authorship. Many modern, academically rigorous readers require the analyst to account for the authorial intention or earliest audience responses surrounding the epistle of James in order to develop modern interpretations of James which they consider conherent and faithful to the ancient text being interpreted. Conversely, the assumptions regarding authorial intention and audience context which one brings to the text color the interpretation of the text substantially. Text, audience, and author share an integral relationship, and each must be taken into account in a rigorous treatment of the others. Thus, an interpretation of James must continue with an

29

attempt to make the assumptions of this study regarding authorship and audience, the other two sides of the triangle, explicit rather than implicit.

One may state assumptions explicitly with either of the following two methods: (1) Description of a specific, known audience and author, and (2) Development of a theoretical construct to serve as a foil against which to read the text. The first method is preferrable whenever it is usable, owing to its advantage for historical reconstruction. The second becomes tolerable when a lack of information makes the first unusable.

Chapter Two

JAMES IN CLASSICAL ANTIQUITY: SOME GENERAL CONSIDERATIONS

The social model of reading enables a reader of James to define the interpretive task with some precision. This model proposes that the author and the reader share responsibility for the formulation of meaning or usage. The written text constitutes a medium of communication, theoretically a concrete artifact with which both the author and the reader grapple, the vagaries of textual transmission notwithstanding. The author, on one hand, and each reader, on the other, bring sets of assumptions and literary conventions to the text. These respective cognitive sets inform the interpretation which the author expects while writing and the concepts which the readers develop when they interpret the text.

In the case of James, the author brought a first century Mediterranean perspective to the text. He lived in a specific cultural milieu and social setting. His audience most likely shared many aspects of this *Sitz im Leben*. At the very least, the author wrote under the assumptions that his self-designation as a "slave of God and the Lord Jesus Christ" would carry some weight with the audience, which, additionally, would respond to its own characterization as the "twelve tribes in the diaspora" (1:1). As we noted above, the author theoretically could have operated within a religious milieu characterized by antagonism to the Pauline slant on the faith-works dichotomy, but the relevant text and comparative material do not lead inexorably to such a conclusion.

The modern reader, in contrast, brings to the text a cultural milieu, social setting, and a set of assumptions informed by almost two millenia of development within the Christian tradition. Many Christian readers, at least, consider the

Pauline formulation definitive and analyze other statements of the faith-works dichotomy by means of comparison to this norm. The cultural milieu is more individualistic than was that of the first century. The rural and urban social lenses through which a modern interpreter might read James differ in many particulars from their ancient counterparts. Thus, the communication process potentially becomes adversarial, with the differences between ancient and modern conditions producing modern readings of James which may or may not be consistent with either authorial intention or early audience response.

A reader may use some degree of circular reasoning to alleviate the inconsistency between authorial intention and modern interpretation. In such an exercise, the text itself provides much of the data to hold in check the modern reader's use of material from his/her own setting to inform an interpretation of the text. Most interpretations of ancient writings perform this function to some extent by incorporating a consideration of the general historical background of the text into the elucidation of the work. In other words, the modern interpreter attempts, insofar as the available evidence permits, to examine the text through the eyes of a hypothetical, usually poorly defined ancient reader. The modern interpreter, however, derives this hypothetical construction largely from an examination of the text under consideration. Thus, circular logic has its drawbacks but still serves a useful purpose in the consideration of ancient texts.

In order to use this circular reasoning technique more precisely, one may examine the text and its backgrounds from either of two perspectives. First, one may learn as much as possible about the author, preferrably from sources other than the text under consideration, and then apply this background to the interpretation of the text in terms of authorial intention. This technique can bring relevant information to bear on the text but requires both a clear identification of the author and the availability of preferrably extra-textual information about that author. Second, in the absence of information permitting the elucidation of authorial intention, one may use specific, extra-textual knowledge about the intended audience to elucidate the text from the perspective of the persons for whom it was intended. The requirements for the use of this technique are comparable to those for the use of authorial intention. The intended audience must be identified, and information about the audience must be available. James, of course, did not identify either himself or his addressees with any degree of precision. Thus, an attempt to interpret the epistle in a manner consistent with its earliest settings requires the reader to identify a hypothetical author or audience, demonstrate the probability that the hypothetical author or audience is similar in key respects to an actual one, and then interpret the epistle in a manner which this hypothetical author or audience would find congenial. To the extent that a reader can incorporate extra-textual information into a hypothetical author or audience construction, the reader can alleviate the pitfalls of using only the text at hand to formulate assumptions which s/he then uses to elucidate the text. This inquiry continues with a consideration of the author's identity, in accordance with Hirsch's preference for authorial intention as the primary factor in the meaning or usage of texts. It continues thereafter with the description of some general characteristics of hypothetical, first century audiences of the epistle.

The Author's Identity

Conservative commentators break the circular chain by equating "James, a slave of God and the Lord Jesus Christ" (1:1) with Jesus' brother James. Davids' two-stage composition hypothesis and L. T. Johnson's cautious support for authorship by Jesus' brother in literate Greek and with recourse to Hellenistic philosophical *topoi* exemplify this position.[1] This exercise enables those commentators to interpret the epistle in light of the information which other ancient writings provide about Jesus' brother. Given Paul's derogatory comments about James (Gal. 2:9-13), the descriptions of their positions in Acts 15 and 21, and the emphasis of several other writings on James' concern for the law and righteousness, this line of reasoning could lead in either of two directions. First, it might reinforce the interpretation of the epistle in light of the Pauline formulation

---

[1]P. H. Davids, *The Epistle of James: A Commentary on the Greek Text* (NIGTC; Grand Rapids, MI: William B. Eerdmans), pp. 12-13, 21-22. L. T. Johnson, *The Letter of James: A New Translation with Introduction and Commentary.* (Anchor Bible 37A; New York/London/Toronto/Sydney/Auckland: Doubleday, 1995), pp. 116-121.

on faith and works. This line of reasoning appears to stem from a dichotomy which Paul established for apologetic or polemical purposes in Gal. 2; the extent to which the dichotomy resembles the actual positions of the two in any other situation remains unclear. Second, it might encourage a reading which focuses on the Torah and the concept of righteousness from either James' supposedly Palestinian perspective or a general, hellenistic cultural point of view.

As most academic interpreters are well aware, the conservative commentators' identification of the author of James with Jesus' brother presents difficulties and certainly proceeds beyond any information which the text of the epistle or any early attestation thereof may provide. The more sanguine interpreters attribute the epistle to a pseudonymous author. Their lines of reasoning follow some aspects of Dibelius' and Ropes' studies. S. Laws, for example, emphasizes the articulate and rhetorically proficient character of the epistle's language, notes the author's preference for the LXX rather than for the Hebrew scriptures, and identifies Hellenistic literary conventions.[2] This line of reasoning leads her to propose a post-Pauline cultural situation, late date, and pseudonymous author for the epistle. E. Trocmé, likewise, interprets the epistle as a response to the difficulties of post-Pauline churches.[3] Other commentators exhibit similar perspectives and conclusions.

Most commentators base their interpretations either on the assumption of authorship by Jesus' brother, with or without the assistance or an amanuensis, or on that of a Hellenistic literary convention of pseudonymity. Two other perspectives, however, are at least theoretically possible. The proposal of authorship by any of the other NT characters named James claims few proponents due to the obscurity or early disappearance of all such characters.[4] The possibility of authorship by an explicitly identified but otherwise unknown author is the least satisfactory for analytical purposes due to its lack of utility. Since the epistle lacks

---

[2] S. Laws, *The Epistle of James* (BNTC; Peabody, MA: Hendrickson, 1980), pp. 40-41.

[3] "Les Églises Pauliniennes vue du dehors: Jacques 2,1 à 3,13," *Studia Evangelica*, 2 (1964), 660-669.

[4] Johnson, *Letter of James*, p.93.

the usual trappings of pseudonymity and the author's name is relatively common, however, one must consider this possibility at least defensible.

The author provides the following two, specific items of self-identification in the praescript to the epistle: his name (Jacob/James) and the designation "slave of God and the Lord Jesus Christ." Previous interpreters have used the proper name, the initial component of the self-designation, to determine possible authors. The fruits of their research epitomize both the benefits and the limitations of this method. On the one hand, they limit the number of possible authors to a handful; on the other, they merely exclude the undesirable possibilities rather than provide a positive identification of the author (cf., p. 9 above). The text itself allows the reader to identify the author with any literate person before the time of Origen who both had the name Jacob/James and might have designated himself plausibly as a "slave of God and the Lord Jesus Christ."

The term δοῦλος occurs only once in James, and the epistle includes no other references to servile status. The author designates himself by reference to this status and then does not return to the concept. In other words, the self-identification in the praescript seems comparable in function to the sender's address at the beginning and the signature, followed by printed name and title, at the conclusion of typical, modern business letters.

The author's self-identification exemplifies a pattern which a modern interpreter, with access to the entire NT and the benefit of hindsight, may classify as a literary convention among the authors of the earliest extant Christian epistles. James is one of several such writers who identified himself as a slave of Christ. Paul characterized himself in this manner at the beginning of two epistles (Rom. 1:1, Phlp. 1:1). One of his successors followed suit (Titus 1:1), as did a later NT author familiar with a collection of Paul's letters (2 Pet. 1:1). Jude 1:1 and Rev. 1:1 attest the popularity of this salutation among early Christian authors beyond the post-Pauline circle.[5] This literary convention apparently fell out of favor shortly after the first four Christian generations, as the authors of the early non-canonical epistles preferred other self-designations.

---

[5]The salutation in Jude 1:1 may constitute an imitation of those in James and/or 2 Peter.

James claimed a servile position in the dominical patronage system but did not specify the exact nature of this position. Paul, in contrast, placed himself at the top of the servile pecking order (1 Cor. 9:17). In one conflict-ridden situation (1 Cor. 9, *passim*), Paul postponed reference to his servile status in order to cite this status as a rationale both for his attempt to resolve disputes authoritatively and for his independence from the support of any patronage system within the Corinthian congregation (c.f., 1 Cor. 1:10-17).[6] James, like Paul, identified an ostensibly conflictual situation among his recipients. However, James used suggestion and understatement to assert his status.

James' self-characterization compares James' status in the Christian community to the status of a slave in an extended family or patronage system. Throughout classical antiquity, this status was conceived in a manner consistent with Aristotle's fourth century BCE generalization: "The slave's sciences then are all the various branches of domestic work; the master's science is the science of employing slaves.... The master must know how to direct the tasks which the slave must know how to execute" (*Pol.* 1:2:23).[7] This identification places James within the metaphorical family or patronage system headed by God and the Lord Jesus Christ. Thus, James argued explictly, though not in a particularly heavy-handed manner, that he wrote as an agent of the deity. In other words, the author expected his epistle to receive a hearing not on account of the author's capability or position but because it carried the divine patron's seal of approval. The citation of servile status constituted an assertion of support from the deity which the author and presumably also the earliest audiences defined as their highest authority.

The initial identification of the addressees confirms the character of the author's self-identification. The author's frequent use of the LXX confirms his

---

[6]D. B. Martin presents this argument in more detail (*Slavery as Salvation: The Metaphor of Slavery in Pauline Christianity* [New Haven, CT/London: Yale Univ., pp. 55-58]) and also summarizes the extensive use of the servile metaphor throughout the NT (pp. 51-54). For more information on the servile pecking order characteristic of classical antiquity, headed by the steward (οικονομος or *vilicus*), see Petronius, *Sat.* 29-30; Columella, *Rei Rus.*; 1:8:2-6; Xenophon, *Oecon.*; 5:16; Cato, *De Ag. Cul.*, 5:1-5; and Varro, *Rei Rus.*, 1:17:1-1:18:4.

[7]Aristotle, *Politics*, tr. H. Rakham (LCL; Cambridge, MA/London: Harvard Univ./William Heinemann, 1990, v. 21, p. 31).

awareness of this scriptural tradition. In the Greek translation, as in the original Hebrew scriptures, the twelve tribes theoretically claimed a common descent from the patriarch Jacob. This common descent, rather than the clan divisions, became a focus of Jewish identity during the first century. With the exception of the hereditary priesthood, distinctions among the twelve lines of descent had receded in importance long before the first century.[8] Ancestral claims and genealogies extending back to the pre-exilic era were exceptional, though not inconceivable (eg., Matt. 1:1-17, Lk. 3:23-38, Rom. 11:1, Phlp. 3:4-6). Jews outside of Palestine frequently congregated in their own areas of Mediterranean cities, with little regard to the specifics of their ancestry. As a result, they characterized themselves simply as Jews and were stereotyped by outsiders in a similar manner.[9]

The tradition of the twelve tribes apparently held symbolic value for James. The distinctions among the tribes represented an allusion to a common history rather than a reference to current distinctions within first century Judaism. Thus, James used this concept as metaphorically as he did the preceding, servile self-designation. The twelve tribes represented for James the totality of the Jewish community; whether the diaspora represented a literal, geographic location; a figurative, social status; or merely a desired sort of self-containment for James is uncertain. Whichever the case, James conceived of his letter as a circular epistle

---

[8]R. Eisenman, *Maccabees, Zadokites, Christians, and Qumran: A New Hypothesis of Qumran Origins* (SPB; Leiden: E. J. Brill, 1983), pp. 7-8, suggests that even the scope of priestly genealogies was limited by the Babylonian devastation.

[9]Many Jewish communities existed as practically self-governing entities within the cities of the Mediterranean basin, with tribal distinctions among the Jewish constituents mentioned scarcely, if at all. Even among the priestly class, genealogies rarely extended as far back as the twelve patriarchs (eg., Josephus, *Vita*, 1:1-6, for a presumably self-serving genealogy from a hereditary priest extending back only to his great-grandfather). For examples of monolithic stereotypes by Jews and others alike, see D. L. Balch, "'...You Teach All the Jews ... to Forsake Moses, Telling Them Not to ... Observe the Customs' (Acts 21:21; cf. 6:14)," *SBL Seminar Papers*, 32 (1993), 369-383. Balch follows his primary sources closely in presuming the character of this stereotype and then examines the treatment by the Romans of the groups identified simply as Jews. The presence of proselytes and God-fearers does not complicate this generalization. Persons with both characterizations were predominantly of non-Jewish ethnic identity, with proselytes converted fully to Judaism (whatever that may have entailed in any given locality) and God-fearers attached more loosely to Jewish groups.

and addressed it to the constituents of all of his communities, wherever they may have been located and whatever their relationships to the surrounding societies. It is unclear whether he and/or his followers considered themselves Jews who also practiced Christian worship, Christians who retained some allegiance to the mother religion, or non-Jewish Christians who had become the true Israel and coopted aspects of their Jewish heritage.

James wrote authoritatively to all of the communities under his leadership. His self-designation as a "slave of God and the Lord Jesus Christ," reinforced his authority by equating opposition to his letter with insubordination to the deity. The equally metaphorical reference to the "twelve tribes in the diaspora" classified the letter itself as a circular epistle addressed to the entire circuit of the author's followers, possibly scattered throughout the Mediterranean basin.

The name Jacob or James was common in some circles during the Roman era. One would assume that there was no question among the recipients regarding which James wrote the letter. Modern interpreters, however, examine the passage from a distance of about two millenia. As the succeeding chapters indicate, Jesus' brother, the most influential of the first century Christians who bore this name, is the candidate whom first-century audiences most likely might have regarded as the implied author, if this concept is anything more than a theoretical construct of twentieth century literary criticism. However, this identification is of limited use. The author identified himself in a manner tantamount to the following salutation: James, writing *ex cathedra*, to his followers throughout the Mediterranean basin. This self-designation is insufficient to permit a clear identification of the author with any NT character named James. Any such identification, no matter how plausible, proceeds beyond both the information which the text itself provides and any relevant information from other ancient sources.

The Epistle in its Cultural Milieu

If an interpreter could identify the author with any person known from other sources, s/he could construct a brief *vita* of the author, propose a plausible hypothesis of authorial intention, and use this information to elucidate the epistle.

This ideal approach would place some limits on the necessity of circular reasoning (ie., the use of a text to construct a hypothesis regarding original setting, followed by the use of the hypothesis, in turn, to interpret the text). This approach is untenable in the case of the epistle. We know only that the author had the common name of James, that he claimed to communicate authoritative instructions, and that he addressed his letter as a circular epistle to his followers scattered in various locations in the Mediterranean basin.

Since one cannot possibly develop a reliable model of authorial intention, reader response provides a fruitful perspective from which to analyze the epistle. One may use information in the text to identify the salient characteristics of the intended audiences, refine this description by recourse to more general information from the relevant chronological and geographic milieux, and use the resulting generalizations as interpretive background for the epistle. This technique does not obviate circular reasoning and its pitfalls. It does, however, enable the modern reader to propose an interpretation which, with some degree of probability, is consistent with the interpretations by some of the earliest audiences. Such an effort, in Jameson's terms, permits a modern reader to remain faithful to the metaphorical contract between author and reader to assure the proper use of the literary artifact within the limits imposed by the chronological and cultural distance and by the scarcity of relevant data from sources outside of the epistle (cf., p. 13).

The inquiry already has classified James, at its broadest level of literary comparison, as a circular epistle. In this respect, the author's expectations regarding its circulation seem comparable to the expectations of the author of the Apocalypse and to the actual circulation of the Pauline *corpus*. The oral performance expectations for such literature provide a ready explanation for the lack of many features of ancient letters; after a brief introduction of the absent author, a lector might read the letter to each congregation almost in a sermonic style.[10] At a narrower level of comparison, the pervasive ethical instructions render Dibelius' generic identification of the letter as *paraenesis* credible but leave

---

[10]The difficulties with Ropes' generic identification of James as a diatribe notwithstanding (*A Critical and Exegetical Commentary on the Epistle of St. James* [ICC; Edinburgh: T. & T. Clark, 1916], pp. 10-16).

open the possibiltiy of refinement.[11] Thus, a reader may identify James simultaneously as an example of the use of authority, a circular epistle, a written guideline for a verbal presentation of prescribed material in a standard rhetorical format,[12] an ethical handbook, and maybe even a loosely organized philosophical treatise (cf., p. 20 above).

This hierarchical arrangement of possible generic identifications suggests a method of determining a possible *Sitz im Leben* for the epistle. One may use the epistle's ethical instructions both as examples of the type of teaching which the author considered necessary for a variety of intended audiences and as indicators of the dilemmas which the author presumed most of his intended audiences would face. This approach refines Dibelius' generic identification by bringing more recent redactional and literary perspectives to bear on the question of definition. The current inquiry accepts Dibelius' description of *paraenesis* as general, loosely organized ethical instruction but then assumes, in contrast to Dibelius, that an author might slant a *paraenetic* work to serve his/her purposes effectively.[13]

James provides extended treatments of socioeconomic distinctions and of verbal sparring. The epistle introduces both topics in its first several verses and then treats them intermittently, occasionally interspersing more general material, until it reaches its conclusion. A superficial examination identifies 1:9-18, 2:1-26, 4:1-10, 5:1-11, and 5:13-18 as possible references to class and status distinctions; 1:19-27, 3:1-18, 4:11-12, and 5:12 as possible references to verbal ripostes; and 4:13-17 as a possible reference to both. More general material of an introductory and concluding character is evident in 1:2-8 and 5:19-20. The author's critical

---

[11]*Der Brief des Jakobus* (KEKNT; Göttingen: Vandenhoeck & Rpurecht, 1921), pp. 4-15. For a recent example of an explicit but cautious refinement of Dibelius' propsed generic identification to increase its specificity, see Johnson's discussion of the similarities between James and the moral discourses of some philosophical traditions (*Letter of James*, pp. 18-22, 27-29). Johnson identifies these similarities as points of contact rather than as a comprehensive set of characteristics which might define a genre.

[12]Summarized in tabular form in L. Thurén, "Risky Rhetoric in James?" *Novum Testamentum*, 37/3 (July, 1995), p. 282.

[13]Cf., L. Perdue, Paraenesis and the Epistle of James," *Zeitschrift für die Neutestamentliche Wissenschaft und die Kunde der Älteren Kirche*, 72 (1981), 241-256.

tone in these passages indicates a treatment based on the assumption that these characteristics were either actual or potential difficulties for the audiences which the author had in mind.

The treatment of economic and social distinctions begins with a surprising evaluation in 1:9-18 of the relative positions of Christians of varying status. The passage instructs the "humble" Christian to boast about his exaltation and the "rich" about his humiliation. The author bases this instruction on the perspective of shared mortality, regardless of status. This warning continues with a paragraph contrasting the person who endures through temptation with the rich person who withers like scorched grass.

The author addresses differential treatment of persons of differing status explicitly in 2:1-26. He criticizes a practice, which he assumes to be widespread among his audiences, of preferential treatment for the wealthy and condescension towards the poor. In vv. 6-7, he identifies his audiences as those who relegate the poor to inferior positions in the church but, in turn, receive similarly condescending treatment from even wealthier outsiders. The section concludes with an argument, followed by an extended example, to demonstrate that such differential treatment contravenes the "law," which he defines as the criterion of conduct to which his churches must adhere.

The problem becomes even more salient in 4:1-10. The author criticizes the audiences' quarrels sarcastically as the way of the world. He contrasts this worldly behavior explicitly with a godly lifestyle. The topic of humility remains evident here, as in the earlier passages, but the contrasting characteristic is modified. This passage emphasizes arrogance or pretentiousness rather than the economic categories of wealth and poverty.

The epistle reiterates the socioeconomic theme in 4:13-5:11. The author accuses merchants of excessive acquisitiveness in a culture characterized by the assumption of limited good and by the use of defensive strategies to preserve prestige and wealth.[14] He continues by lambasting the absentee landlords who

---

[14]For a summary of limited good and defensive strategies to preserve status and wealth, see B. J. Malina, *The New Testament World: Insights From Cultural Anthroopology* (Atlanta: John Knox, 1980).

refuse to pay their free labor as promised. The passage concludes with an admonition to be patient, presumably in contrast to the socially unacceptable acquisitiveness described in the preceding verses.

The emphasis on class and status divisions culminates with 5:13-18. In this passage, the author prescribes confession and healing rituals apparently available across the board, without regard to class or social status. The example of Elijah reinforces the admonition to be patient rather excessively acquisitive.

The admonitions concerning verbal riposte occur throughout the epistle. At least two such warnings are extensive in character. 1:19-27 urges the listeners to listen carefully and to speak and become angry only with deliberation. The classification of failure to control one's speech adequately as immoral, sacreligious, and a failure to "become a doer of the word" (1:22) indicates the emphasis which the passage places on this moral imperative.

An extended treatment of the tongue in 3:1-18 implicates verbal riposte in the audiences' internal competitions for status. The teachers, apparently a group of some status and with public speaking responsibilities, receive a warning that they will he held to especially strict standards. After an analogy demonstrating the difficulty of controlling one's speech, the passage equates wisdom with humility and contrasts acceptable behavior with epithets. Shortly after this treatment, 4:11-12 warns against slander, and 4:13-17 criticizes not only the merchants' acquisitiveness but also their boastfulness, presumably in the struggle for levels of prestige consistent with their economic well-being. The association of verbal riposte with struggles for economic and social standing reaches its culmination in 5:13-18 as the author makes confession and healing rituals available to all by specifying verbal rituals at which presiding personnel need have only the honorific, age-related, or possibly quasi-official, status of elder.

The extensive treatment of economic and social distinctions and repeated warnings about verbal riposte provide important data regarding the conditions which the author expected the epistle's audiences to encounter. The author presumed that he was addressing churches which might benefit from warnings against the abuses related to socioeconomic and rhetorical inequality. How realistic was this presumption? If the author had identified addressees in specific cities, one could interpret these warnings in light of specific social and cultural situations. In other words, one might shed light on the epistle by equating the author's presumed audiences with supposedly actual audiences. Such audiences, though hypothetical, at least would be described in terms of specific data from the inhabitants of the relevant chronological, cultural, geographic, and social locations. Such a procedure would provide an impression of the extent to which the epistle provides an accurate reflection of the situations to which it was addressed.

Since the epistle lacks sufficient information to permit the specific identification of its actual audiences, one must proceed in a more general manner. The following two options are available: (1) The use of a modified, inductive approach, discussing the characteristics of several societies from classical antiquity and then drawing a conclusion on the basis of the bulk of the examples, and (2) Recourse to modern, theoretical descriptions of such societies to draw tentative conclusions about the character of such societies in general. The first option carries a high probability of data selection in light of a previously drawn conclusion. The second option also is amenable to selective use. In addition, this approach necessitates the assumption that the general depiction drawn from a modern synthesis is similar in key respects to a particular ancient example. This second option is preferred because it carries built-in safeguards. Modern, synthetic descriptions of ancient cultures in general were written with an agenda broader than the interpretation of James in view; in fact, most such descriptions do not cite James at all as a supporting example. In addition, information from the object of inquiry provides an indication of the extent to which the epistle's *Sitz im Leben* does or does not resemble the characteristics of the modern synthesis. Thus, an examination of some modern theoretical approaches to the salient characteristics of societies from classical antiquity views a wide range of ancient societies and their primary sources through the lens of several modern interpretations. This technique enables the modern interpreter to determine tentatively the probability of the assumption, evident in James, that warnings about the evils of socioeconomic stratification and abusive verbal riposte were necessary for a large cross-section of the author's followers.

JAMES IN CLASSICAL ANTIQUITY

Sociological and anthropological descriptions of the societies of classical antiquity provide complementary views of the general cultural milieu in which James was written. Both sorts of descriptions lend themselves to generalization, with most of the sociological descriptions exhibiting primarily cross-cultural, structural perspectives and most of the anthropological, in contrast, exemplifying cultural specificity and functional orientation. At some point, inductive approaches provide the mechanisms for theoretical development in both approaches. The successful application of both orientations requires the examination of multiple examples, the notation of their similarities for use as bases of comparisons, and the determination of general conclusions on the basis of the comparison.

G. E. Lenski's investigation of agrarian societies provides a notable, recent example of a sociological approach to the analysis of ancient cultures. Lenski states his concept in explicitly cross-cultural terms, comparing certain characteristics of several ancient and medieval empires. Owing to the availability of data, the Roman Empire, the largest of the concentric political entities in which James arose, provides a fair amount of material for Lenski's analysis. Since this material does not include any substantial consideration of James, the theoretical construct provides a presumptive description of some eonomic, political, and social conditions typical in the epistle's milieu.

Lenski describes agrarian societies in terms of the following eight characteristics.[15] First, such societies exhibit advances in military and productive technology. Second, they control millions of square miles of territory. Third, they include large populations, frequently hundreds of millions of subjects. Fourth, they achieve control of such large populations by means of conquest or forcible subjugation. Fifth, they usually have monarchial forms of government. Sixth, they provide settings for the development of commerce and trade. Seventh, they include widespread urban communities with areas of high population density. Eighth, they provide opportunities for the development of a diversity of occupations and methods of making a living.

---

[15]*Power and Privilege: A Theory of Social Stratification* (Chapel Hill, NC/London: Univ. of North Carolina, 1984), pp. 190-191.

44

The use of these eight characteristics as bases of comparison clarifies the scope of the entities under examination but does not rule out the inclusion of diverse groups within the classification. The similarities noted above enable one to distinguish these empires from more primitive horticultural and more advanced industrial societies. In this respect, the social characteristics simply exclude the clearly unsuitable candidates for classification as agrarian societies and thus supplement the chronological progression which Lenski's typology presumes.

The Roman Empire during the first century CE exemplifies all eight of the characteristics noted above. The applicability of the characteristics, however, serves as an initial and quite general indication that the empire as a whole is amenable to classification as an agrarian society. The extent to which this identification facilitates the analysis of the empire's components and artifacts depends on the distillation of the characteristics into a more concise, theoretical description of the function or structure of the empire and its constituents. Lenski provides such a tool with his description of the social pyramid characteristic of agrarian societies and their constituent entities.

Communities within agrarian empires typically included urban areas and the surrounding rural regions under their sway. The populations of such communities frequently included a very small percentage of social and economic elite who derived the greatest benefit from the economic production of the lower classes. At the top of the social pyramid stood the rulers, numerically the smallest class in an empire. This class enjoyed the most comfortable lifestyles in ancient cities. The rulers relied heavily on the usually indigenous governing classes, with the latter comprising no more than about two percent of the population. In return for the cooperation of the local elite, the rulers frequently provided grants of land, status, and wealth.[16] On the other hand, power struggles between the imperial rulers and the governing classes occurred frequently.[17]

---

[16]Lenski, *Power and Privilege*, pp. 219-230. Lenski apparently models this aspect of his description on M. Weber's concept of rule by *honoratiores* (*Economy and Society: An Outline of Interpretive Sociology*, ed. G. Roth & C. Wittich; tr. Roth, Wittich, *et al* [Berkeley/Los Angeles/London: Univ. of California, 1978], v. 2, pp. 1009-1010.)

[17]Lenski, *Power and Privilege*, p. 231.

A primarily urban retainer class mediated between the rulers and the governing class on the one hand and the common people on the other. In most communities, no more than about five percent of the population belonged to this class. As Lenski's term suggests, this class survived primarily by providing the commodities and services required to maintain the comfortable lifestyles of the rulers and the governing class.[18] Lenski included merchants and priests among the retainer classes. Merchants frequently came from the lower classes, with some servicing the lower classes and remaining poor while others became wealthy by providing luxury items for the upper classes. In this respect those merchants who serviced the rulers and govering classes helped those classes expropriate the bulk of an area's economic surplus and thus garnered a share of the resentment directed towards the upper classes.[19] The priests functioned in a variety of manners in different empires but generally benefitted from and defended the centripetal character of the economic and social conditions.[20]

The vast majority of the inhabitants of any city and its surrounding agricultural areas were peasants and urban artisans who lived at a subsistence level. Most of the artisans were recruited from the ranks of peasants, and many were worse off economically than were the peasants.[21] Generally, peasants might own small plots of land, but artisans owned only their own tools. Below these two classes were the unclean and the expendables. Such classes might include low-status agricultural slaves who populated several synoptic parables and whose roles the Roman gentleman farmers described in detail as well as free, landless persons, such as those who hired themselves out as day laborers in Matt. 20:1-16.

Lenski describes the roles of various classes in agrarian societies in structural terms, though with some attention to function. His model emphasizes the positions which the various classes occupied in the pecking order and provides some explanation of the roles which they filled. His modern emphasis on

---

[18] *Ibid.*, pp. 245-246.

[19] *Ibid.*, 249-252. Such a stereotype of the merchants who serviced the upper classes is evident among first century Christian writers in Rev. 19:11-19.

[20] *Ibid.*, pp. 257 ff.

[21] *Ibid.*, pp. 266-279.

economic characteristics at the expense of social factors and roles probably is excessive for ancient cultures.[22] This emphasis stands in contrast to the careful distinction between social and class status which M. Weber drew throughout his discussions of ancient societies.[23] In spite of this possible drawback, however, Lenski's synthesis stands as an especially coherent example of a detached perspective on the ways in which large, urban population centers in various empires distributed resources and roles among their inhabitants.

Lenski notes that downward mobility was more common than its upward counterpart in classical antiquity.[24] In this one instance, he pays some attention to the ramifications of the socioeconomic system for the individual participant. This observation brings into sharp relief both the advantages and the drawbacks of Lenski's model. On the one hand his description of the positions and roles of classes and large population groups within agrarian societies illustrates the structure of such societies clearly. On the other, his description provides only suggestive material about the ways in which constituents of these social groups might behave towards each other in the various situations typical of classical antiquity. In short, Lenski's view from above becomes even more informative when one introduces a complementary, equally rigorous view from within to elucidate those aspects of social interaction which are not salient when the society is considered solely in terms of Lenski's model.

Several anthropologists have developed a model of social interaction in traditional Mediterranean cultures. This model of limited good develops naturally from the assumption, held to be common in classical antiquity, that all economic and social commodities existed in finite quantities. The model provides an

---

[22]In spite of this difficulty, economic components did influence other aspects of the prevailing social conditions considerably. Weber emphased economic and political analysis throughout *Economy and Society*. For a thorough analysis which is based on Marxist assumptions and which cites James on occasion to make its points, see G. E. M. de Ste. Croix, *The Class Struggle in the Ancient Greek World from the Archaic World to the Arab Conquest* (Ithaca, NY: Cornell Univ., 1981). For a more conservative analysis, see M. I. Finley, *The Ancient Economy* (Sather Classical Lectures 43; Berkeley/Los Angeles: Univ. of California, 1973).

[23]Explained in *Economy and Society*, v.1, pp. 302-307.

[24]*Power and Privilege*, pp. 289-292.

heuristic framework for the analysis of certain behaviors described in societies organized along the lines which Lenski's agrarian model suggests. In short, Lenski's model provides a tool for the evaluation of the larger socioeconomic picture in classical antiquity. Subsequently, after the social context has been established, the model of limited good and related concepts provides a framework for a wide variety of behaviors within such societies.

Lenski developed his structural model by examining cross-cultural data of a large quantity and variety. His presentation of the characteristics of agrarian societies alone encompassed large states and empires throughout Asia and Europe from early classical antiquity through the medieval period. His entire work, like Weber's compilation, included the consideration of societies in virtually all regions of the world from the earliest historical period until the twentieth century. In this respect, Lenski constructed his agrarian model clearly as a cross-cultural type.

The anthropologists who studied individual behavior and social interaction in the Mediterranean basin, unlike Lenski and Weber, formulated their models in light of culturally specific observations. They considered written materials from the area's ancient cultures and readily observable behavior among the current inhabitants. Owing to their presumptions regarding the persistence of the region's traditional cultural norms during the past two millenia, they classified their ancient and modern data as representative of a single cultural milieu.[25] Specifically, they attributed the similar behaviors reported in ancient writings and observed among current inhabitants to the persistence of an ancient, agonistic (conflict-oriented) framework of cultural norms and expectations in many parts of the Near East.

---

[25]For a theoretical perspective, see R. C. Webber, "Recent United States-Iraqi Relations in Light of Traditional Near Eastern Cultural Norms," *Explorations: Journal for Adventurous Thought*, 10/4 (summer, 1992), 45-66, particularly pp. 46-50 for a discussion of Saddam Hussein's superimposition of modern political structures and techniques over the traditional cultural framework. For a less theoretical application of this assumption to the interpretation of the Lucan parables by modern, Near Eastern peasants, see K. E. Bailey, *Poet and Peasant* and *Through Peasant Eyes: A Literary-Cultural Approach to the Parables of Luke* (Grand Rapids, MI: William B. Eerdman's, 1976/1980), 2 vols. in 1 (combined edition), particularly *Poet and Peasant*, pp. 30-37, for a discussion of his conclusions regarding the persistence of traditional cultural norms in the rural areas of the Near East.

The distinctive characteristics of the conflict-oriented social norms become salient in contrast to some aspects of modern, Western societies. Most twentieth-century, middle-class Americans and Europeans assume the availability of adequate commodity supplies to ensure their comfortable lifestyles. Such readers generally earn adequate income to provide clothing, housing, and food for their families. Experience has taught them that such items are available at reasonable prices in retail establishments of various sorts. Consequently, such readers become accustomed to social systems with the following three characteristics: (1) The prominence of economic conditions, (2) Individualism, and (3) Cooperation to accomplish various objectives. The recent downfall of the Eastern European and Soviet communist regimes, which were predicated on a theory of economic conflict, reinforces this pervasive Western perspective.

Traditional Mediterranean societies valued social over economic conditions and emphasized conflict and corporate identity. To return to our previous example, most modern Western readers make daily observation of the adequate availability of life-sustaining commodities, and this constant experience defines the American and European economic system. Most ancient Mediterraneans, in contrast, made daily observation of the stratification reflected in the data from which Lenski developed his model of agrarian societies. Such persons experienced life situations in which a few elites controlled the lion's share of the resources from the surrounding rural areas and used the resources for their own benefit. Consequently, they found the availability of social and economic commodities tenuous at best. As a result, constituents of traditional Mediterranean cultures probably would have found the salient characteristics of modern Western cultures inconsistent with the empirical reality which they experienced on a daily basis.

The agonistic model of social interaction provides a framework for the analysis of behavior within groups such as Lenski's agrarian societies. This model draws not only from the analysis of ancient societies but also from the direct observation of the traditional Mediterranean cultures which continue to thrive in many areas of the Near East. As Lenski drew from diverse sources to prepare a synthetic model of the agrarian social type, B. J. Malina availed himself of a variety of anthropological sources and theories to synthesize a model of social interaction within agrarian societies and other groups characterized by the limited or unpredictable availability of commodities.[26]

Malina's model begins logically with the concept of *limited good*. This modern, theoretical construct of Medieterranean anthropology generalizes the ancient assumption that "all the desired things in life, . . ., exist in finite, limited quantity and are always in short supply."[27] Malina includes within this generalization not only the economic commodities which modern societies value but also socially determined characteristics, such as honor, prestige, and status. To the modern American, and, to a lesser extent, European, goods and services are available in almost infinite quantity, with only the individual's economic resources limiting his/her acquisitions. Thus, traditional Mediterraneans downplay the social and economic advancement for which modern Westerners strive.

Since all commodities exist in limited supply, traditional Mediterraneans consider substantial economic and social improvement unlikely in the best circumstances and impossible in the worst. Thus, traditional Mediterraneans prefer defensive to overtly acquisitive strategies. They usually lead transparent lives in an effort to assure others that they do not intend either to borrow from or to encroach upon the economic and social status of any other individual or family.[28] Owing to this assumption of limited economic and social mobility, traditional Mediterraneans generally tolerate autocratic regimes as long as the rulers do not infringe upon the subjects' subsistence or inherited class and social status.[29]

One might expect the assumption of limited good to discourage competition for resources. This, however, is not the case. Limited good simply restricts competition to clearly delineated social spheres. Traditional Mediterraneans, whose societies exhibit pronounced stratification, identify social superiors and inferiors easily. Competition with persons in either group most likely would not enable one to gain economic or social commodities. On the one hand,

---

[26]Malina, *NT World*, passim.

[27]*Ibid.*, p. 75.

[28]*Ibid.*, pp. 76-79.

[29]*Ibid.*, p.77. For a modern example from a related theoretical perspective, see Webber, "Recent United States-Iraqi Relations," pp. 49-50.

competition with social superiors usually is unsuccessful; on the other, winning a competition with a social inferior usually does not provide any resources to which the protagonist lacks access.[30] Thus, the inhabitant of a traditional Mediterranean society may increase prestige or wealth by participating successfully in the socially prescribed games of challenge and riposte against persons and groups of roughly equivalent socioeconomic status.

Competition for economic and social resources, within the limits imposed on both sides by the probability that the competition will culminate in successful acquisition, defines social interaction within traditional Mediterranean societies. This characteristic is consistent with the assumption of limited good. Since all resources are available in finite quantities, and every individual and group tries to maintain its inherited status and wealth, one can increase his standing by competitive more often than by cooperative means. Thus, Mediterranean societies emphasize competition, an activity which modern Western societies prefer to relegate to athletic and certain corporate endeavors.

Owing to the prominence of social criteria, rather than of economic, in traditional Mediterranean societies, Malina follows most anthropologists in identifying honor and shame, its converse, as the commodities which such societies value most highly, at least among males.[31] He defines honor succinctly as "a claim to worth along with the social acknowledgement of worth."[32] One may gauge the extent of each individual's honor by both the prestige of any groups to which the individual might belong and the position of the constituent within the pecking orders of these larger groups. The individual, of course, might belong to a kinship group (clan), village or town, city or empire (by way of citizenship) and several voluntary associations simultaneously. In most cases, traditional Mediterraneans consider relatives honorable. Constituents of their own small, secondary groups (eg., villages, voluntary associations, etc.) are dishonorable until proven otherwise, with various rituals and tests intended to reverse this social distancing process.

---

[30]J. Pitt-Rivers, *The Fate of Shechem or the Politics of Sex: Essays in the Anthropology of the Mediterranean* (Cambridge/London/Melbourne/New York: Cambridge Univ., 1977), pp. 6-11.
[31]*NT World*, pp. 25, 30.
[32]*Ibid.*, p. 27.

Strangers of the same cultural group become potential enemies, and foreigners are certain enemies.[33] Thus, competition and distrust pervade their societies.

An individual might obtain a grant of honor either by ascription or by acquisition. Ascribed honor simply is the inherited honor of one's clan particularized by the status of the individual within the family. One obtains acquired honor, as the term suggests, in games of challenge and riposte against social equals from other families. The person who initiates such a game of one-upmanship does so by means of an action or verbal exchange intended to call another's honor into question. In most cases, the person so challenged responds with a counterchallenge. As a result, games of challenge and riposte escalate rapidly, as participants strive to save face and increase their prestige. Such games may culminate with physical affronts, the most extreme of which is the killing of one's competitor in a game of challenge and riposte.

One may conduct a round of challenge and riposte in a more cooperative manner. Gift-giving, debates, arranging marriages, various sorts of cooperative ventures, and other activities provide opportunities for all participants to increase their honor to some extent.[34] Within this context, hospitality provides a notable occasion for host and guest to enhance each other's honor in the eyes of each participant's peers. M. Herzfeld, in fact, identifies hospitality rather than honor as the primary commodity of traditional Mediterranean societies.[35] V. H. Matthews describes a longstanding protocol of hospitality which enables host and guest to enhance the honor of one another. Since the guest ultimately leaves the host's sphere of influence, they play their game of challenge and riposte in a manner which does not bring them into direct competition with each other.[36] The successul conclusion of the controversy over the Iraqi government's detention of Western civilians before the 1991 war exemplifies this type of competition. When

---

[33]Malina, *NT World*, p. 33.

[34]*Ibid.*, pp. 32-33.

[35]"'As in Your Own House': Hospitality, Ethnography, and the Stereotype of Mediterranean Society," in *Honor and Shame and the Unity of the Mediterranean*, ed. D. D. Gilmore (Washington DC: American Anthropological Assoc., 1987), pp. 86-88.

[36]Hospitality and Hostility in Genesis 19 and Judges 19," *Biblical Theology Bulletin*, 22/1 (spring, 1992), 3-11.

G. Bush held S. Hussein accountable for the treatment of the "hostages," he presumably intended his statement as a threat. Hussein considered it a reminder of the obvious responsibility to "guests" in his culture and thus as an attempt to help him increase his honor in a cooperative manner. As a result, the detainees left Iraqi confinement safely before the beginning of the hostilities.[37]

The example of Hussein brings into focus another aspect of honor in traditional Mediterranean societies. Groups, like individuals, have various degrees of honor. In fact, given the assumption that the personality is dyadic and embedded in the group (in contrast to Western individualism), the collective dimensions of honor may be the more important.[38] Hussein presumably discharged his responsibility to his "guests" in an attempt to increase not only his own but also his country's honor. Thus, the prestige of the entire nation was contingent on that of Hussein, its head-of-state. This collective dimension of honor provides a partial explanation for the Iraqi public's support of Hussein during and after the seemingly abortive war. From a less theoretical perspective and in a microcosm, Bailey uses a Lucan parable to illustrate the expectation that a Near Eastern village would use hospitality to preserve and enhance its corporate honor.[39]

This cursory overview of the agrarian and the agonistic models of traditional Mediterranean societies demonstrates the compatibility of the two models. The agrarian model provides a general, structural description of imperial economies and societies. This description emphasizes the extreme stratification prevalent in such cultures and situates the epistle in a time and place in which a few persons were haves and the majority were have-nots in both an economic and a social sense. The agonistic model describes the activities by which the constituents of such societies attempted to exploit their limited opportunities for social and economic advancement. One may apply the agonistic model to non-agrarian societies of a traditional sort. The susceptibility not only of portions of the NT but also of the earlier narratives from Genesis and Judges and the more recent dispute between the Bush and the Hussein administrations demonstrate both the

---

[37]Webber, "Recent United States-Iraqi Relations," pp. 54-56.
[38]Malina, *NT World*, pp. 51-60.
[39]*Poet and Peasant*, 120-124.

persistence of the model and its applicability to a variety of social groupings. Thus, the agrarian model informs the analysis of the larger context to which the epistle was addressed, and the agonistic model informs the analysis of the economic and social transactions which the author presumed would take place among his audiences within this larger context.

The Addressees Within the Recipient Churches

The theoretical framework articulated above elucidates the interpreter's understanding of the specific persons to whom the author addressed the epistle. In other words, the epistle includes sufficiently direct addresses to various groups to shed light on some aspects of the presumed audiences' *Sitze im Leben*. The nature of those not addressed also informs the analysis. The epistle includes not only direct addresses to some groups but also discusses other groups as outsiders who are relevant to the recipients' situations but are largely outside of the church.

The epistle addresses economic classes within the churches explicitly at several points. This dichotomy appears initially in 1:9 ff, the contrast of "humble" with wealthy Christians. The contrast refers to both groups as insiders, promises advancement to the poor, and warns the wealthy of their mortality. This line of reasoning continues in 2:1 ff, though the addressees have changed. This subsequent passage accuses those who preside at the assembly of showing favoritism to the rich. Again, however, both the poor recipients of condescension and the rich recipients of favoritism are presumed to be active members of the recipient communities. The arrogance of those who purchase commodities abroad with the intention of selling them at a profit receives criticism in 4:13-17 comparable to that to which rich recipients in general are subjected in 1:9 ff. The criticism of this group calls to mind Lenski's description of those merchants who enjoyed some measure of prosperity by providing luxury items for the elite and the governing classes. The author reserves his most vituperative rhetoric, however, for the "rich" who refuse to pay the wages of their free, hired labor. This group apparently includes church members whose primary assets are agricultural holdings. The author's presumptions that their cash enables them to promise and then withhold wages and that their holdings are sufficiently extensive to require the retention of hired labor suggest identification of these addressees as local elites with inherited wealth and leisure.

The epistle addresses wealthy merchants and large landowners explicitly. In addition, it addresses not only rich and poor Christians in general but also those who preside at the audiences' assemblies and exhibit condescension towards the poor and favoritism towards the rich. Three other economic groups, in contrast, receive mention as strata with which the recipients are familiar but which remain outside of the church. Those who are wealthier than the church members are accused of oppressing the Christians, particularly in judicial settings (2:6-7). The free laborers cheated out of their just wages are on the periphery, and the free farmer with a subsistence-level plot of land serves as a distant, objectified example of patience which requires little explanation (5:7).

The epistle addresses the wealthy quite explicitly. One non-economic group also receives extended, less than congratulatory treatment. Those who wish to become teachers receive an extended warning about the evils of uncontrolled speech (ch. 3). This warning leads directly to a treatment of conflicts among the recipients (ch. 4). Apparently, teachers comprise a high status group among the addressees, and abusive rhetoric arises in the competition for such honor.

In summary, the author of James addressed the epistle to the most highly privileged representatives of his urban churches. Well-to-do merchants and absentee landowners, of course, lived in the cities. These groups represented Lenski's retainer class and, in the context of the Roman Empire, probably the local governing class respectively. Those who wanted to be teachers, like the merchants and landowners, were accused of misconduct in the contest for prestige and privilege. The urban elite, whose status and wealth exceeded that of the specific addressees, were identified as the very rich outside of the churches (2:6-7). Those who spent most of their time outside of the city walls, likewise, were not represented among the addressees. The author acknowledged the presence of the urban poor within his audiences, but only to the extent that their consolation served as a foil for his criticism of the higher status groups.

James addresses precisely those groups which one might expect to find as economic and social elites in agrarian cities. The letter to these groups is largely condemnatory in tone. The author criticizes such recipients for their attempts to increase their status; in this respect, he espouses the defensive strategy preferred in the agonistic model. He advocates the preservation of such groups' inherited status rather than the prominent use of conflict-based techniques to increase status. Only one potentially high-status group does not receive criticism. The elders simply are available to pray and annoint the sick (5:14). Perhaps one could not achieve the status of elder by agonistic means; such status, based primarily on age, was honorific and at most quasi-official.

The low-status groups, in contrast, receive no criticism. In fact, the poor Christians receive the promise of exaltation at the hands of their divine patron. Likewise, the subsistence farmer is praised as an example of the patience which the author advocates for his followers as an alternative to conflicts over wealth and status. Hired laborers, though considered outsiders to the recipients' churches, at least are to be paid properly and protected from the wealthier, more pretentious church members' machinations.

The epistle places its recipients economically and socially. It identifies its primary targets as those church members who enjoy wealth or status and go beyond the normal defensive strategies in their attempts to increase their wealth and honor. Such recipients, as one might expect, live in cities. Some of the elite constituents are identified as the merchants who serviced the needs of their cities' elites, and others are absentee landowners, possibly representatives of the local governing classes just below the Roman or other elites.

The epistle does not situate its recipients geographically. The behavior which it criticizes accords closely with the relevant sociological and anthropological models. Such behavior might be expected among the constituents of any voluntary association in any city of the Mediterranean basin. Thus, recent modifications of Dibelius' definition of *paraenesis* are well-founded. As Dibelius noted, this type of ethical exhortation had its general qualities. However, as several more recent commentators have argued, the generic identification does not rule out all specificity (cf., p. 40 above).

At first glance, James apparently shares little with Paul, the synoptics, the Johannine school of thought, Ebionism or the representatives of early Catholicism. It includes some emphases which might find congenial receptions among any of these groups and others which would engender their hostility. The criticism of competition for status and wealth, for example, is evident in Paul, Revelation, Acts, the synoptics, later Ebionism, and a variety of other works. The use of the Abraham tradition is equally widespread, though the various Christian and Jewish writings of the era utilized the tradition in differing manners. The types of Christian communities which might have found James most or least useful remains open to debate. We know only that the author and/or recipients used Greek as a *lingua franca*, and this observation sheds little light on the recipients' geographic and social locations within the Roman Empire. There is no reason to associate James closely with any other, well-known strand of first century Christian tradition.

The epistle may have viewed some issues differently from the major, written first century Christian traditions. Nevertheless, the successors of these other schools of thought preserved and ultimately canonized the epistle's perspective. Thus, at some level, these other Christians found the epistle informative. Given the subsequent development of Christianity, colored heavily by the emerging prevalence of the post-Pauline tradition, one must include post-Pauline churches among those which found a measure of utility in the epistle. In other words, Jacobin thought could be conformed to Pauline ideology in a manner plausible to the societies described above. If James had countered Paul in an especially consistent, effective, or obvious manner, the third and fourth century heirs to the post-Pauline tradition would have found little reason to preserve James as an authoritative component of their canon.

This inquiry has come full circle. James provides only general information about the nature of its recipients and the situations to which it was addressed. We cannot describe an original Jacobin audience with much specificity. Thus, we must create hypothetical but plausible first-century audiences in order to determine some ways in which the epistle may have been read during that era. Owing to the influence of the post-Pauline audiences in the preservation of the epistle, and in order to facilitate the contemplation of a probable role for those audiences, the next chapter describes such an audience on the basis of some of its own literature and then reads the epistle as the audience might have. The following chapter provides a check on the post-Pauline perspective by reading the epistle from an explicitly Jewish-Christian point of view. Neither of the audiences described below actually existed in antiquity, and the exact configurations of the two interpretations, like the audiences on which they are based, are ideal types suitable for analytical purposes rather than for exact historical reconstruction.

Chapter Three

JAMES IN A HYPOTHETICAL, POST-PAULINE MILEU

In a broad sense, any reading of James by a modern, Christian audience constitutes a post-Pauline interpretation. Virtually all current strands of Christianity trace major doctrines to the Pauline influence. Thus, representatives of these faith communities interpret early Christian writings by using assumptions developed through two millenia of the post-Pauline interpretive tradition. In other words, virtually every Christian perspective filters James through the lens of the Pauline tradition. The differences among the modern perspectives stem from any other lenses through which the readers might filter their analyses of James.

As the preceding chapters indicate, this inquiry has classified the post-Pauline interpretation of James more narrowly than the parameter described above might suggest. This reading makes conscious use of information about the literary conventions and socioeconomic conditions of the Pauline churches and their successors to establish a background for the elucidation of James. In other words, this inquiry reads James in a manner which a late first or early second century CE post-Pauline audience might have found plausible in some respects. The audience, as a theoretical construct, provides only a basis for the approximation of culturally and historically probable readings rather than an indication of actual interpretations during antiquity. In other words, the reader response method, circumscribed by culturally specific limitations, sheds light not on the epistle's early circumstances but on the sorts of receptions plausible among some readers in the decades after its composition. This perspective, in sum, is culturally specific in comparison with the generally Pauline orientation of most traditions within modern Christianity.

Before reading James in post-Pauline terms, one must describe the hypothetical, post-Pauline audience to which the interpretation refers. Of course, this activity depends heavily on the Pauline/post-Pauline corpus, thus providing a readily available limit on the use of circular reasoning. However, before one may delineate a post-Pauline audience, he must determine a point of departure for the endeavor. As in the preceding description of some social characteristics common in classical antiquity, one could begin with primary sources, a procedure which would leave open the possibility of data selection in service of a previously determined hypothesis. This potential pitfall is particularly salient in the case of a corpus notable for its sheer familiarity and quantity. The opposite procedure, that of beginning with secondary sources, provides no more random data selection than does the use of primary sources. This other procedure, though, limits the possibility of selective data usage by bringing into consideration biases and principles of selection concerned primarily with Pauline rather than with Jacobin issues and interpretations.

One may begin either at the theological or at the socioeconomic end of the ideological spectrum when delineating the contours of a post-Pauline audience. In either case, the audience, as defined above, occupies a chronological position towards the end of the first or beginning of the second century CE. The genuine Pauline epistles, Colossians/Ephesians, and the pastorals may prove relevant. We cannot be sure which components of the Pauline corpus any specific church possessed in its collection. In addition, the improbability of the attribution of the latter two groups of writings to Paul is more readily apparent to modern audiences with two millenia of hindsight than it was to their first century CE predecessors.

E. P. Sanders' approach to Pauline issues suggests an organizing principle which impinges on both ends of the ideological spectrum. Sanders' consideration of the ways in which one may obtain and retain the status of an insider in good standing enabled him to examine both the theoretical and the practical aspects of "patterns of religion."[1] An extensive analysis of a wide variety of literature which

---

[1] *Paul and Palestinian Judaism: A Comparison of Patterns of Religion* (Minneapolis: Fortress, 1977), pp. 17-18.

Jewish groups wrote or preserved during classical antiquity led to the conclusion that the various strands of Judaism adhered to a pattern which he called "covenantal nomism." This pattern emphasized the belief that insider status and, ultimately, salvation, depended on God's mercy rather than on human achievement. More specifically, God chose Israel and promulgated the law, which implied the requirement of obedience and sanctioned the requirement with the threat of punishment. In addition to this stick, however, the law included the carrot of atonement by which a severed covenantal relationship might be restored.[2] As a result, various versions of Jewish faith and practice held in common the belief that adherence to the law constituted the *sine qua non* of group identity. The versions distinguished themselves only by specifying different emphases in their definitions of acceptable compliance with the law.

Paul, in contrast, considered Torah observance neither a necessary nor a sufficient condition for faith and practice. Sanders identified this position as the definitive difference between Pauline thought and that of the Jewish writings which he analyzed. Paul considered Christ the necessary and sufficient condition for salvation, which the believer might appropriate through faith. Therefore, for Paul, Torah observance served a merely pedagogical purpose for Christians of Jewish background and was antithetical to Christian identity for converts of Gentile provenance.[3] Sanders thus characterized Judaism and Pauline Christianity, in spite of some common, covenantal characteristics, as incompatible patterns of religion and parted with those predecessors who had emphasized the continuity between the religious traditions.[4]

The post-Pauline churches had recourse to two epistles in which Paul used his interpretation of Gen. 15:6 as a prooftext to buttress his definition of Christian identity. In Gal. 3:1-25, Paul contrasted works of the law with faith (v. 2), cited

---

[2]Sanders, *Paul and Palestinian Judaism*, pp. 422 123.

[3]*Ibid.*, pp. 518-519. Before describing this distinctive aspect of Paul's thought, Sanders notes some covenantal aspects similar to typical Jewish thought (*ibid.*, pp. 511-515).

[4]The most thorough example of this earlier perspective on Paul, and one which Sanders critiqued repeatedly, is W. D. Davies, *Paul and Rabbinic Judaism: Some Rabbinic Elements in Pauline Theology*, 2nd ed. (London: SCM, 1955).

Gen. 15:6 to characterize Abraham as an example of salvation by faith (v. 6), and then identified Christ as heir of the promise to Abraham, which promise preceeded and superseded the law. In Rom. 4:3, he cited the same prooftext both to defend his theory of justification by faith apart from works of the law and to introduce his argument that Abraham was the forefather not only of the Jews but also of many nations, a point which he reiterated in Rom. 9. Thus, Paul used the example of Abraham in Gen. 15:6 to defend his formulation of acceptable faith and practice in two divergent settings.[5]

When Paul had his way, observant Christians of Jewish background could find a home in his churches, and those of Gentile provenance also could find a home without being required to observe the law. In Romans, at least, non-Christian Jews, though misguided, also inherited the Abrahamic covenant.[6] The example of Abraham in Gen. 15:6, as interpreted by Paul, emphasized the principle of Gentile inclusion but did not leave out the other groups. Galatians, in fact, indicates a competition for status among protagonists of the two cultural groups to which Paul conceded insider status, with the Jewish Christians pressing for prominence by way of uniform adherence to their standards of faith and practice as a condition for full fellowship.

Paul spelled out the ethnic and theological parameters of acceptable faith and practice primarily in Galatians and Romans. In other epistles, Paul emphasized the ethical and social aspects of this concern. Recent essays by G. Theissen, collected from various sources and reprinted in book form, explore such dimensions of corporate identity in one church to which Paul addressed himself at length.[7] In spite of Theissen's emphasis on economic rather than social standing, his essays on 1 Corinthians provide a useful description of the conflicts which

---

[5]J. S. Siker, *Disinheriting the Jews: Abraham in Early Christian Controversy* (Louisville, KY: John Knox, 1991), pp. 72-76, argues that Paul used this basic formulation in Galatians to discredit the efforts of Jewish-Christian teachers to require of Gentile Christians a more Jewish form of faith and practice and in Romans to address the relative status of non-Christian Jevos and Gentile Christians in a less polarized situation.

[6]*Ibid.*, p. 75.

[7]*Studien zur Soziologie des Urchristentums*, 2er aufl. (Tübingen: J. C. B. Mohr [Paul Siebeck], 1983), theoretical and Pauline essays reprinted on pp. 3-76, 201-330.

apparently riddled one of Paul's churches and of Paul's proposals to ameliorate the conflict within that church.

Theissen's theoretical and analytical foundations stemmed from conflict-oriented concepts of society similar to those articulated by Lenski and Malina. Theissen devised a theoretical framework which emphasized the role of conflict in social development, classifying activity into the following four categories: 1. Domestication: the internalization of social restrictions, 2. Personalization: the adaptation of society to take into account the characteristics of human nature, 3. Compensation: the avoidance or illusionary resolution of conflict, and 4. Innovation: the occurrence of social development as a result of actual conflict.[8] His analytical foundation lends itself to more concise summary than does his theoretical framework. On the basis of a prosopography of the names in 1 Cor. and/or Acts 18, Theissen concluded that Paul's Corinthian congregation included both rich and poor constituents.[9] *"Wenn Paulus nun sagt, es gebe nicht viele Weise, Einflussreiche und Vornehme in der korinthischen Gemeinde, so steht ja eins fest: dass es einige gegeben hat."*[10] Thus, Theissen depicted Paul's Corinthian church as a group with a lower-class majority led by a wealthier, more pretentious minority.

After establishing his theoretical and analytical foundations, Theissen provided an economic reading of Paul's instructions regarding two conflicts within the Corinthian congregation. He interpreted the dispute over the propriety of eating meat offered to idols as a difference of opinion between the poor and the wealthy church members. The wealthy, on the one hand, could afford meat and had ample social opportunity to eat meat from the temple butcher shops. The poor, on the other, were limited on most occasions to vegetarian subsistence diets.[11] Theissen subsequently read the instructions for the Lord's Supper as

---

[8]"Theoretische Probleme religionssoziologischer Forschung und die Analyse des Urchristentums," rpt. in *Studien*, p. 62.

[9]"Soziale Schichtung in der korinthischen Gemeinde: Ein Beitrag zer Soziologie des hellenistischen Urchristentums," rpt. in *Studien*, pp. 234-257.

[10]*Ibid.*, p. 234.

[11]"Die Starken und die Schwachen in Korinth: Soziologische Analyse eines theologischen Streites," rpt. in *Studien*, pp.279-289.

recommendations to end the use of this ritual as a traditional banquet at which the leaders exhibited their high class and social status by providing each participant with food and seating directly proportional to his status.[12] This practice engendered resentment comparable to that which many literate clients expressed regarding aspects of ancient patronage systems. Theissen concluded his work with a new essay interpreting Paul's christologies as reflections of the possibilities of social advancement in the urban societies of classical antiquity.[13]

Theissen's work demonstrates its utility in spite of two methodological assumptions which can be sustained only with difficulty. Theissen made uncritical use of the data from Acts 18 and emphasized economic stratification anachronistically at the expense of the social distinctions which were equally important in classical antiquity. Nevertheless, his depiction of the Corinthian schism, when modified to account for social as well as economic stratification, demonstrates an impressive consistency with both the sociological and the anthropological models of ancient society. Theissen argued repeatedly that Paul advocated a benevolent patriarchialism by supporting the practices of the Corinthian elite theoretically but then instructing them to make allowances to avoid offending church members of lower socioeconomic status.

The brief examination above provides an outline of some contours of Pauline church characteristics. This sketch obviously makes selective use not only of data from the Pauline epistles but also of modern interpretations of Paul. The principles of selection derive from the preceding overview of James. The two primary principles are the use of Abraham, particularly of Gen. 15:6, as an example of the proper relationship of faith and works and the presence of socioeconomic stratification within the church. Furthermore, the Pauline literature provides no reason to propose any relationship between these two principles. These examples suggest the need for attention to the works of Sanders and Theissen, and this choice of modern interpreters, in turn, colors the portrait of Paul and his churches.

---

[12]Soziale Integration und sakramentales Handeln: Eine Analyse von 1 Cor. 11:17-34," rpt. in *Studien*, pp. 302-317.

[13]"Christololgie und sociale Erfahrung: Wissenssoziologische Aspekte paulinischer Christo-logie," *Studien*, pp.318-330.

A post-Pauline audience which conducted itself in the terms outlined above would organize itself along the lines of ethnic identity and socioeconomic status. Such a congregation would use the example of Abraham, particularly Gen. 15:6, to demonstrate that God was the father, at the least, of Gentile and Jewish Christians if not also of non-Christian Jews. The congregation, in short, would emphasize its discontinuity rather than its continuity with Judaism.[14]   In addition, the congregation would exhibit a traditional, hierarchical pattern of social roles. The influence of the prevailing norms and deutero-Pauline and pastoral *haustafeln* would overshadow Paul's instructions regarding concessions for the benefit of Christians of lower status.[15]

Ethnic and socioeconomic differences may have created problems for some Pauline and post-Pauline churches. Paul, however, kept the categories separate conceptually in his writings. He used the example of Abraham at length only in letters to the Galatian and Roman churches in which the issue of ethnic identity was paramount.   When instructing his Corinthian followers to alleviate socioeconomic tension, he found no use for Abraham. Likewise, his successors, who articulated visions of social propriety in terms of traditional formulations, did not refer to any of the standard Abraham prooftexts. For these post-Pauline writers, the resolution of the ethnic dispute and the dominance of Gentile Christianity limited the utility Abraham as an example of faith and practice. Thus, the assumption that the example of Abraham was irrelevant to socioeconomic practices constitutes the final characteristic of the hypothetical, early post-Pauline audience through whose ears we strive to hear the epistle of James.

A Post-Pauline Reading of James

The salient characteristics of a hypothetical, Pauline audience include a concern for the proper position vis-a-vis Judaism, the citation of Abraham as an

---

[14]Sanders, of course, takes this approach. His straw man Davies, *Paul and Rabbinic Judaisrn*, emphasizes the continuity between Jewish and Pauline thought.

[15]See, for example, D. C. Verner, *The Household of God: The Social World of the Pastoral Epistles* (SBLDS 71; Chico, CA: Scholars, 1983).

example to defend the Pauline perspective on the ethnoreligious question, and the prominence of intramural divisions occasioned by socioeconomic stratification. Paul's letters indicate that not every congregation faced every issue, but this compilation of Pauline topics similar to some Jacobin concerns provides a focus for the subsequent reading of James. Actually, the deutero-Paulines and the pastorals suggest that the ethnoreligious question receded in importance gradually during the post-Pauline era as Gentile Christianity developed a dominant position. In addition, the post-Pauline writers reinforced conservative social practices, more in keeping with Paul's assumption that an imminent eschaton would eliminate the practices than with his concern for the divisive effects of some such practices.

For our hypothetical, post-Pauline audience, the Pauline and post-Pauline correspondence constitues the primary comparative material, since the audience is defined in temls of its familiarity with this material. The audience, after all, is an artificial, theoretical construct and is useful only to the extent that it elucidates possible late first century readings of James. The content of James itself suggests audience familiarity with additional materials. The author cites the LXX repeatedly, and several passages suggest the possibility of familiarity with a tradition of dominical sayings similar to that preserved in the synoptics.[16] Other writings from classical antiquity provide suitable illustrative and comparative material, but one cannot presume audience familiarity with these writings. In fact, given the limited literacy rate and circulation of written materials before the advent of the printing press, it is likely that most first-century audiences had recourse to limited selections of documents.

The initial salutation of James identifies the composition as a letter in a format familiar to post-Pauline audiences. This format, in fact, is similar to that of the Pauline, deutero-Pauline, pastoral, and many non-Christian salutations.[17] The

---

[16]L. T. Johnson, *The Letter of James* (AB37A; New Yorlc/London/Toronto/Sydney/Auckand: Doubleday, 1995), pp. 56-57, cf., S. Laws, *The Epistle of James* BNTC; Peabody, MA: Hendrickson 1980), pp. 35-36.

[17]For numerous examples of ancient, non-Christian letters, which remain informative in spite of their limited geographic provenance and the compiler's overly fine distinction between literary epistles and non-literary letters, see G. A Deissmann, *Licht von Osten: Das Neue Testament und die neuentdeckten Texte der hellenistisch-römischen Welt*, 4en aufl. (Tübingen: J. C. B. Mohr

letter format brings to mind the vehicle which Paul and his successors chose for authoritative instructions to their churches, and the servile metaphor also reinforces this impression and reflects Pauline usage. Thus, the salutation conveys the impression that the letter carries pronouncements regarding the preferred manner of conducting of the church's affairs during the author's absence.

The salutation identifies the intended audience as the twelve tribes in the Diaspora (1:1). The author does not indicate whether the description characterizes the recipients as Jews with a Christian veneer, Christians of Jewish background, or Gentile Christians who coopted aspects of Jewish identity. In any case, however, the description emphasizes those aspects of the recipients' identity which might support claims of continuity with Judaism. Thus, the salutation gives the post-Pauline audience an immediate indication that the letter, though familiar in format, represents a perspective which differs from that of Paul.

Within the obvious epistolary framework, the content and form of the letter permit any of several plausible structures, or even the possibility of no structure.[18] L. T. Johnson's suggested organizational principle represents a pragmatic method of dividing the letter topically for heuristic purposes. This arrangement identifies the first chapter as a précis to introduce the topics which subsequent chapters elaborate.[19] This proposed arrangement is adequately unsophisticated to be comprehensible in a typical ancient setting in which the epistle was read aloud rather than disseminated in print. Under this proposal, the salient topics introduced in ch. 1 and expanded in chs. 2-5 include testing/perseverance, wisdom, economic favoritism, and verbal riposte.

Testing and Perseverence

After the salutation, the epistle opens with a brief passage about testing or temptation and its result, patience/perseverence (1:24). The letter reiterates these topics later in the introduction (1:12-15) and subsequently recapitulates the latter

---

[Paul Siebeck]), pp. 116-213.

[18]For a summary of possible approaches, see Johnson, *Letter of James*, pp. 11-15.

[19]*Ibid.*, pp. 14-15.

topic, as exemplified by the subsistence farmer, the prophets, and Job (5:7-11) immediately before the conclusion. The limited attention which the epistle devotes to this pair of topics suggests an emphasis below that accorded to wisdom, economic favoritism, or verbal riposte.

James uses the πειρα- word field to describe testing. Paul's use of the same concept provides adequate material to clarify our hypothetical audience's frame of reference. In a passage on marriage, Paul equates the urge to conduct oneself immorally, a possibility if a couple were to abstain from sex for legitimate reasons, as a temptation by Satan to violate prescribed behavioral norms (1 Cor. 7:5). In his brief, haggadic midrash on the Exodus narrative, he describes the Israelites as a poor example which his listeners should not emulate (10:6, 11-12). After noting the disloyal behavior of the Israelites and its unpleasant consequences, he warns his audience not to test Christ as the Israelites had tested the Lord (10:9). Following this admonition, he argues that God will allow only the typical, human temptations and will provide a way out of such situations (10:13). Paul does not address the possibility or lack thereof that God might serve as the source of such temptations. Thus, in 1 Cor. 10, Paul uses the concept of testing or temptation with reference to a loyalty test. He admonishes his followers not to subject the deity to such a test and promises that their loyalty to the deity will be tested by the normal patterns of life in such a way that they might withstand the test and maintain their affiliation successfully.

Paul's use of the concept in Gal. 6 also emphasizes the relational aspects of the concept of testing. In this brief passage, Paul contrasts both sin and testing/temptation (v. 2) with carrying each other's burdens, considering one's own works, boasting without slighting another, and carrying one's own load (vv. 4-5). In this same passage he equates testing implicitly with inflated self-importance and comparison to others. This train of thought remains evident in 1 Thess. 3, where Paul equates the successful conclusion of a test with the church's maintenance of loyalty to him and his colleagues in spite of their difficulties. The analogy of 2 Cor. 13:5, likewise, compares the consideration of one's own status in the faith to a loyalty test such as those implied in the other passages.

A deutero-Pauline author used the concept of testing or temptation in the same manner as did his predecessor. In 1 Tim. 3:5, this author equates testing with a desire for financial gain. He includes this assertion in an entire passage criticizing some recipients' use of the church to increase their own wealth. He blames these constituents for inducing strife in the church (vv. 3-5) and recommends a defensive strategy of satisfaction with one's inherited wealth (vv. 6-10).

Paul's usage of the concept of testing or temptation resembles that evident in other early Christian and Jewish writings. His exposition of the Exodus narrative follows the original in using the concept with reference to the loyalty tests to which the divine patron and the Israelites subjected each other.[20] The synoptics, likewise, describe the testing of Jesus in terms of social transactions with human opponents and the devil.[21] This pattern continues well into the ante-Nicene period. In most contexts, the concept of testing exhibits a negative connotation and receives criticism. In summary, the brief, inductive consideration of some early Christian usage does not exclude other possible interpretations but does reveal the substantial usage of this concept in a quasi-metaphorical sense.

Paul and his successors conceived of the concept of testing by analogy with loyalty tests and defensive social strategies. The analogy of the loyalty test becomes apparent in situations involving persons of unequal social status. That of the defensive strategy is more salient in social transactions between parties of roughly equal status. The NT writers use the concept in these ways frequently, not only when one person or being tests another but also in exhortations for individual listeners to test themselves.

One may explicate the transactional concept of testing readily in terms of the agonistic characteristics of ancient Mediterranean societies.[22] In such societies, each individual and group had some degree of ascribed (inherited) honor.

---

[20]See, for example, the usage of this concept in the LXX of Gen. 22:1, Ex. 17:2, 20:20, Num. 14:22, Deut. 8:2, Jdg. 2:22, Is. 7:12, Ψ77:41, 1 Macc. 2:52, and Jud. 8:25-27.

[21]See, for example, Matt. 4:1, 6:13, 16:1, 19:3, 22:18, 22:35, 26:31, Mk. 1:13, 8:11, 10:2, 12:15, 14:38, Lk 4:2, 4:13, 8:13, 11:4, 11:16, 20:23, 22:28, and 22:40.

[22]For an overview of these characteristics, see pp. 47-54 above and B. J. Malina, *The New Testament World: Insights from Cultural Anthropology* (Atlanta: John Knox, 1981).

Social transactions with outsiders facilitated the acquisition of additional prestige but also held the possibility of unsuccessful outcome. The honor of a group and of its head frequently were interdependent. Societies characterized by the assumption of limited good discouraged overly aggressive methods of acquiring honor and preferred less ambitious attempts to preserve the individual's or the group's inherited status and to increase this ascribed honor modestly.

The transactional concept of testing fits into this social model conveniently. When a person put the deity to the test, this behavior challenged the honor of a being who was a social superior by definition. The deity, of course, had the power to punish the impudence of the human subordinate doing the testing. On the other hand, the deity, as a social superior, could test the loyalty of his followers at will. Such behavior simply encouraged the divine patron's clients to remain loyal and provide the socially prescribed deference. Testing oneself or another person of roughly equal status was analogous to a typical game of challenge and riposte, with the activity validating the social status of the participants.

The relational characteristics of testing and perseverence in an agonistic culture inform the reading of these topics in the epistle. Immediately after the salutation, the author urges the audiences to "consider it a joyful matter when you should undergo various tests" (1:2). He bases this command on the assumption that the testing of their faith will bring about the positive results of perseverence, maturity or perfection, and no substantial liabilities (1:34). This brief passage details neither the specific nature of the tests nor the manner in which they might bring about the desired results.

The dyadic social psychology of traditional Mediterranean groups suggests a possible understanding of the tests and their results.[23] Ancient Mediterranean cultures, such as those which Malina described, emphasized group affiliation and construed individual identity in terms of the person's embeddedness in a kinship or other group. The vestiges of this orientation, in fact, remain evident in some modern, Near Eastern societies. Thus, in a dyadic context, faith represented group affiliation to a larger extent than it did an individual's belief system.

---

[23]For a more detailed description, see Malina, *New Testament World*, pp. 51-70.

Maturity/perfection and the lack of substantial liabilities, likewise, had strong social connotations which might not be familiar to modern westerners with highly individualistic orientations.

The social dimensions of testing and its desired results suggest a frame of reference for the interpretation of the epistle's introductory statement. A post-Pauline audience, living in an agonistic culture which valued suspicion and held an orientation such as that described above, would have construed testing as either a game of challenge and riposte or an inspection by a social superior to determine the strength of the individual's embeddedness in the Christian community. Success in such a test predictably would enhance perseverence, construed as loyalty, with this primary virtue becoming evident in mature, socially prescribed behaviors defensiveness/transparency, and a lack of substantial liabilities.

James 1:12-15 elaborates the reasoning which the previously discussed passage introduces. Loyalty or perseverance in the test, equated with "loving him [the divine patron]," results in the bestowal of the crown of life. Since the listener already was an insider to the Christian group, this reward was comparable to the modest promotion with which a human patron might reward a loyal servant or client within the pecking order of the patron's retainers.

The conceptual framework might suggest the following two construals of the test: A loyalty test or inspection by the divine patron, and a game of challenge and riposte between the Christian and a social equal. The passage disallows the first of these alternatives. Only a social superior may conduct a loyalty test, such as the trials during the exodus, as interpreted in 1 Cor. 10. Consequently, the evil one lacks the social standing to test God's loyalty, and God has no motive to reduce his status by initiating a game of challenge and riposte with a social subordinate. Conversely, the author asserts that God will not test his followers. Even though God, as a social superior, could test the loyalty of his followers, this proposition maintains his social distance. The assertion reinforces God's status as patron and the standing of all listeners as clients at various levels by eliminating the possibility of a game of challenge and riposte between a believer and the deity. Given the hierarchical nature of the culture and the necessity of approximate social status for games of challenge and riposte, this argument eliminates the prospect of testing or temptation by the deity by means of *reductio ab absurdum*.

The author construes testing by means of analogy with games of challenge and riposte. He identifies the Christian's equal partner in these games as the Christian's own desires, a logical analogy among those with dualistic and dyadic orientations. In abstract terms, when such desires win the game, they create the possibility of "sin," that is, of rude, crude, and socially unacceptable behavior. This behavior leads to the opposite of the crown of life, the obvious metaphor for which is death. Thus, the epistle interprets failure in the test and sin as the individualistic, self-promoting behaviors which counteract the emphasis on group solidarity.

The passages on testing/perseverence in ch. 1 explain the prominence of group rather than of individual identity in abstract, theoretical terms. They accomplish this task by attributing self-serving behaviors to testing. They understand testing in a manner analogous to games of challenge and riposte and removing the deity from the testing game entirely. In other words, the testing of insiders is presented as a potentially divisive practice, and the testing of the divine patron is labelled as an example of highly impudent behavior by social subordinates. Likewise, the patron does not test his followers, as this function resides more properly with outsiders and with the normal events of life. Consequently, the deity is removed entirely from the testing game. These passages do not provide specific instructions regarding the socially responsible behaviors which James preferred; more detailed instructions of this sort occur at other points.

After the author provides such instructions, he returns to the topic of perseverence, the most salient result of undergoing a test successfully. He uses three brief examples to summarize the social characteristics of the behaviors which he considers socially responsible (5:7-11). Immediately after a condemnation of the dishonest practices of wealthy landowners, he cites the patience of the subsistence farmer as an example worthy of emulation. In ancient urban settings, such farmers held a relative low social status and were vulnerable to a wide variety of economic dislocations. Thus, the author instructs his listeners to behave like a certain type of low-status individual rather than to compete with each other and hold grudges. On a more positive note, the prophets, noted for their perseverance through hardship, and Job, who survived a series of explicit loyalty tests, received veneration surpassing the social promotions which the audiences might expect. The promise of the Lord's imminent return enables the author to postulate an occasion on which the divine patron will give his retainers the rewards of higher status which they might earn with loyalty and socially responsible behavior.

Wisdom

A few centuries after the NT materials were written, J. Stobaeus prepared an anthology which compiled sayings from various sources into a Stoic handbook of practical ethics. Towards the beginning of this anthology, he included an aphorism which differentiated wisdom, that is, the discernment of truth and falsehood, from technical expertise.[24] His distinction neither reflects a Jewish or Christian milieu nor serves as background for the treatment of wisdom in James. Nevertheless, the distinction seems consistent with the social milieu of urban areas during earlier centuries, since it introduces sayings from virtually all chronological portions of classical antiquity. In addition, the distinction mirrors the treatment which wisdom received in the Pauline and post-Pauline correspondence.

Lenski's structural model of agrarian societies (pp. 44-47 above) provides a rationale for the distinction between wisdom and technical expertise. According to this model, urban artisans occupied a low position in the pecking order of ancient cities. In the best cases, they were slightly better off than were free subsistence farmers. Thus, the ancients valued leisure and considered work and technical skill at best necessities for the survival of the majority (eg., 2 Thess. 3:6-13). Paul apparently took his Corinthian audience by surprise when he worked for a living rather than accepting material support from the wealthier among his Corinthian followers. This practice identified him as a person of limited status and leisure but also enabled him to avoid the obligations which the acceptance of a patronage relationship and a dole from those followers might have entailed.

---

[24]*Ioannis Stobaei Anthologium*, ed. C. Wachsmuth & O. Hense (Berlin: Weidemann, 1884-1923), v. 1, p. 18.

Many of the writers who disparaged the lower classes and claimed for themselves some measure of wisdom, in contrast, were well-to-do. Plato and his companions, for example, represented the Athenian socioeconomic elite. Their villas, material resources, and leisure time permitted them to discuss the sometimes arcane, sometimes practical topics included in the dialogues. Plato's student, Aristotle, became a tutor to the Macedonian royal family. Several centuries later, the Roman emperor M. Aurelius wrote a series of philosophical meditations from a Stoic perspective. In short, many philosophers discerned an integral relationship between wisdom, on the one hand, and social prestige and comfort, on the other. This generalization receives some validation from the thorough critique to which it was subjected by the Cynics' itinerant lifestyle and ideal of *apatheia*.

The disribution of wisdom terminology in the Pauline epistles illustrates the socioeconomic connotations of the concept. With the exception of two brief references, one in Rom. and the other in 2 Cor., Paul restricted his use of the terminology to the initial section of 1 Cor. This epistle, taken as a whole, emphasizes the socioeconomic dimensions of Christian community, and the section with a concentration of references to wisdom (chs. 1-3) introduces Paul's condemnation of schisms and cliques within the congregation. The use of the wisdom terminology apparently contributed to Paul's denunciation of the persons and practices which had been reported to him and had incurred his disapproval.

After the salutation and introduction of schisms as a topic, Paul used a substantial portion of ch. 1 to contrast his practices with the wisdom which he attributed to his opponents. In an apparently sarcastic vein, he claimed that he baptized and preached without recourse to wise words (1:17), characterized the foolishness of the cross as the opposite of wisdom (1:18), and cited Is. 29:14 to ridicule the wisdom of his wise followers (1:19). He concluded this section with a rhetorical question to the effect that God had made the wisdom of this world tantamount to foolishness (1:20). After an interlude (1:21-31), Paul resumed this line of reasoning in a less sarcastic vein in ch. 2. In v. 14, he explained his preference for fear and trembling rather than sophisticated, persuasive words of wisdom. He intended his strategy to ensure that his followers place their faith in God's power rather than in human wisdom (v. 5). Likewise, v. 13 distinguished spiritual matters from human wisdom. In these passages and in the citation in 2 Cor. 1:12, Paul gave a highly negative connotation to wisdom by associating it with the baptism rituals binding followers to leaders in the church's cliques.

Paul clarified his negative opinion of his opponents' wisdom by contrasting it with divine wisdom. In 1 Cor. 1:21-31, he equated divine wisdom with the ostensible foolishness of his gospel. He noted that few of his followers were wise, powerful, or well-born by worldly criteria and then argued that God had shown a preference for their opposites, the foolish, the weak, and those born into low status (vv. 26-28). Paul expected this preference to lead to a social situation in which deference to the deity's wisdom, justice, sanctity, and redemption would replace the typical self-promotion (vv. 29-31). He suggested that if the gospel had been communicated in a manner consistent with the standards of wisdom, the elites of this world would have recognized its character and would not have crucified the object of his proclamation (2:8). The isolated citation in Rom. 11 :28-36 exhibits a similar type of comparison. In this passage, Paul reflected upon the extent to which the deity's wealth and wisdom surpassed that of his Roman audience.

The post-Pauline writings retained the concept of wisdom as a divine bequest. Eph. assumed this analogy (eg., 1:8, 1:17, 3:10) but also conceptualized wisdom as practical, ethical guidelines. This latter characterization became more salient in Col. (eg. 2:23, 4:5) though the patronage analogy remained strongly evident (eg., 1:9, 2:3, 3:16). Ironically, Paul's successor, unlike his model, taught with wisdom (1:28). Clement of Rome's first epistle to a Corinthian church echoed themes from Paul's letters to his churches in the same city. In many cases, Clement elaborated the socio-economic dimensions of wisdom which Paul had addressed with less specificity. In 13:1, for example, Clement identified the wise, strong, and rich in terms reminiscent of those in which Paul had addressed the wise, powerful, and well-born in 1 Cor. 1:26. In a particularly telling passage (38:5), Clement contrasted the strong with the weak, the rich with the poor, and the wise with the lowly rather than with the foolish. The last of these three comparisons juxtaposed the wise with the same social class with which Jas. 1:9-11 contrasted the rich. Paul, on the other hand, usually compared the wise to the foolish rather than to the lowly. Clement's exhortation that the wise demonstrate their wisdom by good works rather than by verbal riposte communicates an instruction remarkably similar to the sentiment of Jas. 3: 13-17.

This brief examination of the use of wisdom terminology by Paul and his successors suggests a generalization of the concept with which some post-Pauline churches might have been familiar. Paul incorporated wisdom into the social structure typical of the cities in which he worked. Persons who wished to attain higher social status might claim wisdom as a means of self-promotion in games of challenge and riposte. Successful performance in the social games might enable them to recruit followers to provide the public deference which, in turn, would validate their claims to wisdom and higher status. Activity of this sort apparently contributed to a situation in which a few church leaders emerged as the competing patrons of various cliques within the church. Church members of lower status became clients and enhanced their patrons' prestige within the church, if not in the larger context of the city's entire, upper-class social network.[25]

Paul retained the concept of wisdom but revised the patronage framework in a more figurative direction. Rather than have each patron and his clients compete against every other patron/client group for status within the church, Paul proposed that his followers of high status consider the deity the entire church's benefactor. This analogy necessitated the attribution of wisdom to the deity and the classification of all believers as his clients. In this analogy, wisdom functioned not as an intellectual but as a social commodity with the potential to influence the public perception of those fortunate enough to have wisdom. Virtually by definition, constituents of status-conscious societies valued favorable public opinion highly. Thus, Paul characterized wisdom as a commodity which the deity might give to his clients, much as a human patron might provide grain or a subsistence allowance for his clients.[26] Consequently, Paul urged those church leaders who claimed wisdom to redefine themselves as the deity's clients rather

---

[25]For an equally cynical evaluation of Augustus' assumption of the role of patron in order to consolidate his power, see Tacitus, *Annals*, 1:2.

[26]For examples of such patronage arrangements, both individual and corporate, see Acts 6:1-7, Lucian of Samosata, "On Salaried Posts in Great Houses," Martial, *Epigrams*, 1:20,1:59, 1:101, Juvenal, *Satires*, 5, 7, 9, and Strabo, *Geography*, 14:2:5.

than as patrons to other church members and to consider wisdom analogous to a grant of prestige from a social superior. Such a grant most appropriately engendered reciprocal treatment, that is, deference in the case of a social subordinate, to call attention to the divine patron's beneficence in ascribing such honor in the first place.

James incorporates the concept of wisdom into a similarly analogical framework. The epistle introduces the topic by sandwiching the brief statement of 1:5-8 between the remarks about testing and the contrast of the rich to the lowly. The author recapitulates this topic in 3:13-18 between an elaborate passage about the evils of the tongue and an explicit criticism of the audiences' internal strife. Thus, James, like Paul and his successors, uses wisdom metaphorically and emphasizes its social rather than its intellectual aspects.

The epistle's initial remarks about wisdom introduce the topic in terms of a fictive patronage system. Any of the listeners who lack wisdom may ask the deity for a bequest of this commodity. The deity, as their patron, will give them wisdom freely and without reservation (1:5). In a relationship between social equals, a gift from one requires reciprocal generosity by the other (cf., Lk. 14:12-14). A patronage arrangement, in contrast, generally presumes material support by the patron in exchange for public deference by the clients.[27] The deity, as patron of all of his followers, provides wisdom to any of his clients who lack that social commodity. His free, unreserved manner of giving contrasts with the ulterior motives and calculating methods by which some patrons provided their clients' subsistence in order to purchase their public deference and the high social standing which such deference might precipitate.

The epistle presupposes that all of its listeners already are constituents of the Christian community. Thus, the patronage system already has been initiated. In both Luke's and Lucian's examples, the prospective patron initiates the

---

[27]For particularly cynical views of such relationships from a literate client's perspective, see Juvenal, *Satires*, #7 and Lucian of Samosata, "On Salaried Posts in Great Houses" (first and third centuries CE respectively). For an idealized view, apparently from a conservative, upper class Christian, see Acts 6:1-7.

relationship by approaching a prospective client who had made himself available.[28] The earlier narratives about the grant of wisdom which Solomon received, likewise, characterize the grant as the divine patron's initiative to renew with Solomon the patronage relationship which the deity initiated with Solomon's father (1 Kings 3:3-14, 2 Chron. 1:7-13). In James, the patronage relationship begins with the believer's entrance into the Christian community. Thus, the listener, as an established client, does not need to wait on the deity to offer a grant of wisdom. The believer may go to the patron directly and make his request. Since the deity can display his resources and prestige by granting the request, as a practical matter, he does not need to exhibit the calculating behavior with which some literate clients stereotyped their patrons.

As the free and unreserved granting of a client's request for a grant of wisdom characterizes the deity's behavior, so making the request either in faith or in doubt characterizes the client's role in the transaction. On the one hand, a client who makes the request with the expectation that it will be granted behaves appropriately to his status. He approaches a social superior with whom he is aligned in a way which enables the superior to display his wealth and generosity. According to many ancient writers, such displays provided the bulk of many patrons' opportunities to increase their public standing.[29] On the other hand, the client who doubts that the patron will grant the request behaves in a manner inconsistent with both his status as an insider in the patron's social network and the norms of the larger society. Such a request is tantamount to a hostile challenge. One might initiate such a challenge properly towards a social equal who is not a member of the challenger's actual or fictive kinship groups. A patron would not meet either of the criteria; he is both a social superior and an insider. Thus, both bases for games of challenge and riposte make a hostile challenge to a patron an inappropriate gesture. James, in accordance with the larger society's norms, assures its audiences that the divine patron will dismiss such impudence by refusing the request and putting the recalcitrant client into his proper place.

---

[28]R C. Webber, "An Analysis of Power in the Jerusalem Church in Acts," unpublished Ph.D. diss. (Louisville, KY: Southern Baptist Theological Seminary, 1989), pp. 150-154.

[29]Webber, "An Analysis of Power," pp. 145-146.

The epistle returns to the topic of wisdom in 3:13-18. In the previous passage, the epistle discussed the availability of wisdom as a grant to any or all listeners from their patron. The current passage, in contrast, addresses itself to those listeners who claim to have wisdom. The passage begins by exhorting the wise to demonstrate their wisdom by performing good works. After a brief consideration of the opposite possibility, the passage concludes by enumerating purity, peacefulness, submission, mercy, impartiality and several other types of behavior which might exemplify a divine grant of wisdom but which frequently were not pragmatic in agonistic cultures (vv. 17-18).

The middle verses of the passage criticize jealousy and ambition. Such emotions and the resulting behaviors frequently were productive in the competition for social standing. In agonistic cultures, the protagonists in social disputes frequently advanced their interests and those of their groups by making progress at the expense of the competition, as might be expected in a society characterized by the assumption of limited good.[30] The epistle argues that, as insiders in the same fictive kinship group, the listeners should not advance their individual interests at the expense of their fellow believers. Such behavior is excessively individualistic in a dyadic society in which each individual is embedded in a larger group.[31] The behavior might facilitate the social advance of some constituents but might call into question the entire group's honor. The epistle attributes internal disharmony and meanness to such self-serving behavior, after castigating the behavior as worldly, physical, and demonic (vv. 15-16). These results of the use of wisdom in power struggles resemble the context in which Paul considered wisdom in 1 Cor. 1-2.

The epistle concludes its discussion of wisdom by contrasting the results of a grant from the divine patron with the results of the wisdom claims used for social advancement. Divine wisdom leads to pure, peaceful, gentle, yielding, merciful, behavior, which, in turn, creates a climate characterized by good, impartiality, and a lack of hypocrisy (v. 17). Such an atmosphere contributes to internal harmony rather than to the acquisition of individual honor. Consequently, those who

---

[30]Malina, *New Testament World*, pp. 71-93.
[31]*Ibid.*, pp. 51-70.

behave in the manner prescribed above make peace for the entire group and enjoy peace and righteousness themselves as a result of their grants of divine wisdom.

Economic Favoritism

Much of Paul's treatment of economic discrimination was implicit in his criticism of his Corinthian church's patronage groupings. However, the hypothetical, post-Pauline audience had recourse to at least one direct polemic. In 1 Cor. 11:17-34, Paul followed up his criticism of the church's internal cliques with a polemic against the manner in which the church observed the Lord's Supper. In a highly critical passage, he accused the participants of participating in their own suppers, becoming drunk, allowing some to go hungry, and humiliating the have-nots (vv. 21-22). After reiterating the tradition upon which his church based its observance, he told them to wait for the other participants before beginning the observance and to eat at home beforehand to eliminate the need for gluttony (vv. 33-34). This passage suggests that Paul responded to reports that the practice of providing different qualities and quantities of food and wine for various parti-cipants had proven divisive. Some participants drank excessive quantities of wine, and others, who arrived late, received no food at all. In any case, Paul presumed that the addressees had homes in which to eat and drink. Apparently, some participants who were guests at the meals left hungry and took offense at the way in which the meals were conducted.

Differential treatment at banquets was sufficiently common to draw the ire of other writers with experiences similar to those reported to Paul. Lucian complained that when he attended banquest, his patron might give him a small, tough bird or a serving of meat with a substantial portion of fat and bones while providing meat of substantially higher quality for more highly regarded guests (On Sal. Posts). Juvenal, a closer contemporary of the NT writers, contrasted the quality of the toadstool which he received at a banquet with that of the mushroom on his patron's dish (Sat. 5). When Martial encountered similar treatment, he toasted his patron with the following wish: "May you eat such a mushroom as

Claudius ate!"[32] Theissen suggests that Paul's criticism of the Corinthian Lord's Supper becomes more comprehensible in light of such practices. Those with the means to provide the supper began their banquet before the elements were consecrated, thus circumventing the requirements of the ritual observance. This practice enabled them to conduct a private feast, with differential portions for representatives of various status groups, and to exclude those who arrived late for the Lord's Supper by running out of food before its consecration initiated the ritual observance.[33] Paul instructed the leaders of his Corinthian congregation to resolve the matter by detaching the private affairs from the Lord's Supper.

Socioeconomic status differences created opportunities for favoritism and discrimination in the cities of the Mediterranean basin long after Paul wrote. Clement of Rome, who wrote two epistles to Corinthian congregations within 75 years after Paul, composed some passages in his epistle in such a manner as to heighten the invective in 1 Cor., which apparently served as his model. The authors of the deutero-Paulines and the pastorals, in contrast to Paul and Clement, downplayed those aspects of Paul's thought in the interest of their conservative agendas. Lucian, who admitted in a satire unrelated to his critique of patronage that he held some degree of respect for the Christians of his era, addressed similarly discriminatory practices about two centuries after Paul wrote.[34]

Ethnic and religious identity, like socioeconomic status, held the potential to create occasions for favoritism in the Christian assemblies of Paul's era. This issue apparently occasioned a crisis in Paul's Galatian congregation after emissaries from James convinced Cephas (Peter) to cease table fellowship with Gentile Christians, with the result that many Jewish Christians followed Cephas' lead (Gal. 2:11-14). The position of this incident in the Galatian correspondence immediately after Paul's description of the agreement which he previously had reached with

---

[32]*Epigrams*, 1:20, tr. W. C. A. Ker (LCL; Cambridge, MA/London: Harvard Univ./William Heinemann, 1943), v. 1, p. 43. Claudius, was assassinated by means of a poisoned mushroom.
[33]"Soziale Integration und sakramnentales Handeln: Eine Analyse von 1 Cor. XI:17-34," *Studien* pp. 290-317.
[34]In "Alexander the False Prophet" (v. 4, pp. 173-254 in LCL ed.), he claimed that only some Christians joined him in recognizing the fraudulent nature of Alexander's claims.

Cephas, James, and John creates the impression that Paul considered the incident a personal humiliation and retaliated in kind by confronting Cephas publicly in Antioch in a high-stakes game of challenge and riposte. Rom. seems conciliatory in comparison with Gal., though the two epistles addressed some of the same issues. Paul argued throughout Rom. that both Gentiles and Jews could lay claim legitimately to full-fledged insider status within the Christian community, thus obviating the rationale for favoritism in table status on the basis of ethnic or religious background. This issue apparently receded in importance for Paul's successors as Gentile Christianity ascended gradually into a dominant position. In any case, the issue does not seem relevant to the Jacobin audiences.

James begins to criticize the favoritism typical of the culture by postulating a level of parity between rich and poor. This emphasis on the economic dimensions of socioeconomic status establishes a pattern, though by no means an exclusive one, for the remainder of the epistle. James urges the lowly to boast about their exaltation and the rich to boast about their humilitation (vv. 9-10). This role reversal stems from the mortality which the two socioeconomic classes share (cf., Ps.-Phoc. 116-121). The subsequent v. 11 notes the sudden and inevitable manner in which a wealthy person will die ultimately. That the poor frequently came to such an end presumably did not require mention, particularly in cities with high population densities, poor sanitation systems, and a steep socioeconomic pyramid. The elaboration of v. 11 suggests to the lowly that mortality is a fact of life which they share with the rich. More importantly, however, the verse warns the rich that, insofar as their mortality is concerned, their status does not differ markedly from that of their fellow-believers of low socioeconomic status.[35]

Later in ch. 1, the epistle reiterates the concepts of the deity as patron and believers as his clients. The deity is identified in vv. 16-17 as the immutable father of lights and the source of all good, perfect gifts. This language reflects the

---

[35]This basis for the lifestyle which the author characterizes as Christian is similar to Seneca's rationale for the philosophical lifestyle in "De Brevitate Vitae," 1:1, though the essay contrasts commoners with the reputable rather than rich with poor and proceeds from a Stoic perspective *Moral Essays*, LCL ed., v.2, pp. 286-287).

deference which any highly placed benefactor might receive from clients or subjects, with the primary frame of reference being the titles with which participants in a wide variety of ancient religions addressed their deities. Owing to the high status ascribed to the deity, virtually by definition, the position of the epistle's audiences as the firstfruits of his creation suggests a proportionately high, status for these groups, as collective honor was thought to reside in the head of the group. This ascription reflects the status of the audiences in a manner comparable to Paul's corporate christology in 1 Cor. 12:12-31 and praises of his congregations in Phlp. 1:3-8 and 1 Thess. 1:2-10.

The critique of favoritism on the basis of economic disparities continues with 2:1-13. The first few verses note the differential treatment which the rich and the poor might have received in the recipient churches. The epistle does not spell out the exact nature of the assemblies, but at least two scenarios are possible. The synoptics placed Jesus in synagogues (the term used in Jas. 2:2) on several occasions, with a focus on the reading and interpretation of passages from the Hebrew scriptures. The scenario in Lk. 4:14-21 and parallels seems typical, with Jesus' healings during appearances in other synagogues marking departures from the norm. The passage in James may refer to similar activities, with the complaint relating to seating proportionate to each participant's wealth at services of the word. Alternatively, the passage in James may refer to discriminatory treatment at communal meals, such the Lord's Supper and the various banquets which the satirists criticized.[36] The first gospel, unlike James, distinguished carefully between the two types of assemblies when it accused Jesus' opponents of desiring seats of honor in both settings (Matt. 23:6).

The use of the term "synagogue" in Jas. 2:2 suggests the context of an assembly for scriptural interpretation. Such a situation is consistent with other usage of the term before it came to designate the building in which the assembly occurred. The example of the rich and the poor distinguished by their different

---

[36]The Pauline and the two synoptic Last Supper traditions (1 Cor. 11:17-34, Lk 22:7-38, and Mk. 14:12-26/Matt. 26:17-30) agree in their presentations of the meal in question as a communal event with some degree of formality. Paul stated, and the synoptic authors implied that the observance served as a model for some of their audiences' communal meals.

types of clothing, however, is more consistent with the setting of a formal meal. In the Matthean setting of the wedding banquet parable, the host had one participant removed owing to his lack of proper clothing (22:13). There seems to be no question regarding the plausibility of this scene; only the refusal of the host's friends to attend and the necessity of inviting guests of all sorts of from the streets stand as surprising elements. In the hypothetical example of Jas. 2:1-7, the rich man's gold rings may exemplify a Christianized version of the exhibition of wealth at cultic meals. The wearing of jewelry may be comparable to the prominent display of luxury items at the Dionysian mysteries' meals (Plutarch, "On Love of Wealth," 527D) or at Trimalchio's feast, which Petronius described as the epitome of conspicuous consumption (Satyric., 29 ff). Trimalchio, the wealthy banquet host in Petronius' satire, wore jewelry which made the gold rings of Jas. 2:2 seem modest in comparison (Satyric. 32). If the audiences of James provided differential treatment at communal meals on the basis of economic status, they adopted a practice reported widely in ancient literature.

The differential seating in the audiences' assemblies potentially portrayed the economic disparities which may have contributed to the development of the Jacobin churches' internal pecking orders. Whether the assemblies were communal meals, such as the Corinthian affairs which Paul criticized, or services of the word, the author warns the audiences against defining status and role within the assemblies on the basis of economic distinctions. Whether or not the audiences actually engaged in such practices is unclear; the text describes the seating arrangement as a hypothetical possibility. The text does suggest, and other extant writings confirm, that such preferential treatment for the rich may have occurred naturally in the epistle's social matrix.

The epistle places the differential seating arrangement explicitly within the framework of honor and shame. The author condemns the practice on the grounds that it dishonors the poor in the same way that becoming a defendant in a court of law can expose one to public ridicule (vv. 6-7). Of course, the poor seldom bring lawsuits and succeed only very rarely. Thus, the epistle stereotypes litigation as the exclusive pursuit of the wealthy. In contrast to the worldly pursuit of litigation, the royal law dictates that one love his neighbor as himself (v. 8), and the law of freedom prescribes acts of mercy (vv. 12-13). Thus, the epistle presents the dignified treatment of the poor within the audience as a component of the proper observance of the law which the Jacobin churches' divine benefactor promulgated. This rationale appears compatible with some of Paul's pragmatic recommendations but foreign to his theoretical orientation.

Public assemblies, presumably held at least every Sunday, provided the most frequent and ostentatious opportunities for the definition of congregational identity in economic terms. James warns against divisive seating arrangements in such assemblies. The epistle also criticizes the regular business practices of the following two classes of wealthy constituents: the merchants (4:13-17) and the owners of large argicultural estates (5:1-6). The parallel treatment of these two groups suggests a logical thought sequence, with the criticism of one group following that of the other naturally.

In Lenski's structural model (pp. 44-47 above), rich merchants and landowners occupied two different positions in the social pyramid. The merchants served as retainers, providing the luxury items which enabled the elite to maintain their lifestyles. Since land was the primary productive resource in agrarian societies, the large agricultural landowners represented the local elite to which the merchants catered. Representatives of both classes could become quite wealthy but enjoyed differing degrees of prestige in agrarian societies. Successful merchants made themselves wealthy by commercial activity. Landowners, in contrast, based their lifestyles on the inherited wealth of their families. Agonistic cultures emphasized a concept of limited good and its corollary, a preference for defensive strategies to acquire moderate amounts of prestige and wealth. Consequently, the landowners, with their inherited resources and status, enjoyed higher status than did the merchants, who necessarily used more aggressive strategies to increase and protect their wealth.

The epistle criticizes the merchants initially and the landowners immed-iately thereafter. This order of presentation exemplifies the rhetorical tactic of escalation. The author begins with an easily assailable target, obtains the audience's support for his agenda, and proceeds to a less susceptible target. In other words, the critique of the merchants brings the previously untouchable landowners within reach of the author's condemnation. Limited good and the insistence on defensive strategies provide common denominators for the negative evaluation of the behavior of both classes.

The epistle criticizes the merchants for traveling to other cities for extended periods of time to do business and turn a profit (4:13-17). This reference seems more suitable for the wealthy purveyors of luxury items than for the less well-to-do sellers of products for local use. The epistle labels the merchants' arrogance inappropriate for their type of work and recommends a dose of humility, based on the realization that they require their divine patron's permission to pursue profit, as an antidote. Both the acquisitiveness and the boasting receive criticism. This hostility towards the wealthy merchants mirrors the more detailed criticism of the same class in Rev. 18:11-18. Since the merchants in agrarian societies provided creature comforts and investment commodities in exchange for the wealth expropriated by the elite, condemnation of their activity by the lower classes fits easily into the socioeconomic framework of classical antiquity.

The author criticizes the wealthy merchants in a perfunctory manner in order to prepare the audience for a more thorough condemnation of the even wealthier, more prestigious landowners (5:1-6). Their misconduct is more severe; the passage accuses them of withholding the subsistence wages of their free labor.[37] Such behavior obviously constitutes an excessively aggressive and dishonest strategy to increase wealth in an agonistic setting. The strategy both cheats the workers out of a fair wage and throws into question the ability of the large landowners to recruit the day labor required to provide large-scale agricultural production and support the population of a densely populated urban area and its environs. Thus, the behavior receives criticism for both ethical and pragmatic reasons related to the agonism of the larger social context.

---

[37]Christian literature, such as Matt. 20:1-16 and Rev. 6:5-6, assumed that agricultural laborers usually received a subsistence wage fior their work and that a higher wage was unusual. These passages did not address the possibility that a landowner might withhold the wages entirely, but such behavior was at least plausible in the urban environs of agrarian societies in which the conditions described by Lenski left the free agricultural labor unorganized and powerless. Ps-Phoc. 19, unlike the NT passages, admonished its listeners directly to pay their laborers. Ecclus. 34:21-22, like James, treated the possibility of non-payment in a hyperbolic manner.

The epistle provides the ultimate sanction to discourage such socially damaging behavior. The passage begins with the promise that the rich landowners are preparing their own destruction at the eschatologicat judgement. This threat results from the landowners' hoarding of wealth and refusal to pay their workers' wages (5:34). Their behavior contrasts with that of their divine patron, who hears the cries of the seasonal laborers. Thus, the landowners' self-serving and luxurious lifestyles simply identify them as the objects of ultimate condemnation. The author makes no secret of his preference for the social solidarity which ancient Mediterranean groups emphasized over the acquisition of wealth by the individual constituents of his congregations.

Verbal Riposte

Two of the passages discussed above indicate the possibility or presence not only of economic favoritism but also of verbal riposte. Jas. 1:9-11 argues that persons at the opposite extremes of the social pyramid share a common mortality. Since death constituted the ultimate dishonor in agonistic cultures, the author of the epistle may have considered the inevitability of this fate a great equalizer. On the basis of this reasoning, the epistle encourages both the lowly and the wealthy to boast, the former in their high and the latter in their humiliated status. Boasting, of course, provided an easily utilized method for games of challenge and riposte. The participant might initiate a game with this method in order to obtain immediate validation or credulity for his claims of enhanced prestige. Thus, the exhortation to boast accords well with the methods used regularly to acquire honor in agonistic societies. The ironic content which the passage recommends, however, makes the typical boasting ludicrous and unlikely to receive widespread validation. The passage thereby facilitates an emphasis upon common humanity rather than on disparate socioeconomic conditions.

Jas. 4:13-5:6 criticizes the overly aggressive strategies which the merchants and landowners use to acquire additional wealth. This passage, in addition, roundly condemns the merchants' boasting about their profitable activities. Keeping the agrarian social pyramid in mind as the two groups receive their criticism, one might envision a situation in which the landowners, with their inherited wealth, occupied a position near the top of the pecking order. The merchants, below the landowners because they are *nouveau riche*, might boast about their status as self-made men in order to contrast their own acumen favorably with that of the class above them. The merchants would engage in this endeavor to obtain validation for their claims of status consistent with their wealth.

The hypothetical, post-Pauline audience would find the discouragement of boasting a familiar topic. Again, Paul's Corinthian correspondence plays a pivotal role in the elucidation of the frame of reference by which the audience reads James. Both 1 and 2 Cor. include passages in which Paul either discouraged or ridiculed the use of boasting to increase status. Paul concluded two adjacent passages about cliques and schisms in the Corinthian church by warning the audience not to boast about their affiliation with any particular leader. After identifying the parties and postulating the reversal of roles among those of high and low status (1 Cor. 1:10-28), he argued that this role reversal would ensure that none would have a basis on which to boast before God (1:29). The alternative to boasting in front of God, of course, was boasting about God (1:31), presumably to outsiders. This latter activity enabled the Corinthian congregation, as social subordinates, to pay the socially prescribed deference to their divine benefactor. In the subsequent passage, Paul downplayed his, Apollos', and Cephas' roles in the Corinthian congregation by comparing them to wage laborers in an agricultural or construction environment (3:1-20). This analogy enabled him to argue that all of aforementioned individuals had contributed to the same project. Even though Paul considered himself a skilled laborer and held this possibility open for the others (3:10-15), the analogy led to the statement that Christ, rather than Paul and his co-workers, was the church's leader. This line of reasoning led logically to the conclusion that the Corinthians had no grounds to boast about their affiliation with the human leaders whose positions were comparable to that of wage labor (3:22-23).

1 Cor. 12 provides additional evidence of a contest for status within the church with some indication that the participants utilized verbal methods in their games of challenge and riposte. This chapter subdivides easily into two sections for analytical purposes. In the first section (vv. 1-11), Paul enumerated several

gifts of the spirit and attributed all of the gifts to the same spirit and the same God. This passage suggests that the various spiritual gifts could validate claims of status, with those who had the gifts competing to determine an order of importance, not only for the gifts but also for the gifted individuals. By characterizing all of the gifts as grants to clients from the same, divine benefactor, Paul minimized the importance of both the gifts and the individuals in the church's pecking order.

This line of reasoning continues with the corporate metaphor (vv. 12-26). Paul compared the church to a human body to demonstrate that the whole depended on all of its constituents and would find any absence or lack of cooperation deleterious. His discussion of the less honorable members which were treated with greater respect (vv. 22-24) provided a response to the possible identification of the opponent as the butt of the joke in both senses. In a surprising role reversal, those members with limited prestige, like the midsection of the human body, required special deference. The second section concludes with a recapitulation of the various roles and spiritual gifts within the church (vv. 27-31). This list clarifies the corporate analogy by urging the congregation to treat the different abilities and functions as complementary and equally necessary roles within the corporate structure rather than as individual differences which might determine the status of each church member.

Paul spent the bulk of 2 Cor. 11 ridiculing the boasting of his opponents. After labeling these persons "hyper-apostles" (v. 5) he produced a catalogue of the punishments and physical dangers which he had experienced during his travels (vv. 23-29). After this list, his boasting in the grants of divine protection, a heavenly vision and the ability to tolerate his infirmities (11:30-12:10) exemplified his previous insistence on boasting about the divine patron as a form of deference. This response apparently was rooted in the disparagement of Paul's refusal to accept patronage from any of his Corinthian followers; those who did accept such material support denigrated Paul for earning his keep or accepting his support from other sources (11:7-15).

Phillipians includes two brief warnings against the use of verbal riposte in the competition for social status. After Paul quoted the hymn of Phlp. 2:6-11, which promised social promotion in recognition of the fulfillment of a servile role, he urged the audience to refrain from grumbling and dissension (2:14). In the next chapter, he cited his credentials as a strong basis for a claim to high status but then dismissed the credentials with a profanity (3:7-11). His alternative to the boasting exemplified his emphasis on his benefactor's rather than on his own status.

James begins its explicit treatment of verbal riposte in 1:19-27 with an warning against anger. This passage urges the audience to listen willingly and to speak and express anger deliberately, since human anger does not mirror the divine patron's righteousness, a dimension of his and the group's collective honor (vv. 19-20). The passage defines keeping one's tongue under control as a necessary dimension of loyal affiliation with this particular patronage system (v. 26). The passage not only discourages anger but also suggests an acceptable, alternative behavior. One might demonstrate his loyalty to the patron by exhibiting the prescribed behavior, that is, by caring for vulnerable constituents such as widows and orphans (v. 27). This alternative behavior constitutes appropropriate obedience to the divine patron's "perfect law of freedom" for the group (v. 25).

This passage suggests that anger and verbal abuse proved their utility in the audience's intramural squabbles. A social superior could use anger and verbal abuse to punish the impudence of a subordinate, who, in turn, could use these methods to put a superior on the defensive. Social equals could use anger and verbal abuse in their contests for increased status. The passage labels such games as inconsistent with the divine patron's beneficence.[38] Material support for the constituents of limited means, in contrast, constituted a more productive demonstration of status and beneficence within the church and also accorded with the prophetic elements of the audience's scriptural tradition.[39]

The treatment of verbal riposte reaches its most explicit point in 3:1-12. This passage warns against an attempt to become a teacher on the grounds that one with such status will receive judgement by an especially strict standard (3:1). After a series of analogies to reinforce the point that the tongue, the instrument of

---

[38]See, Johnson, *Letter of James*, p. 205.

[39]Acts 5:1-7 and Strabo, *Geog*, 14:2:5 make the same point in narrative form, regarding a hypothetical, ideal church and the Rhodian civic polity. Tacitus, *Annals*, 1:2, provides a cynical opinion of one emperor's use of this practice to consolidate his power and public support.

speech, can do damage out of proportion to its size, compared to the rest of the body (vv. 3-8), the author notes the incompatibility of deference to the divine patron and verbal abuse of the patron's other clients (vv. 9-12). Participants in agonistic cultures, of course, consider outsiders the proper objects of verbal abuse, as this activity can enhance prestige in a competitive environment.

This passage provides an especially clear picture of a major sort of power struggle against which the epistle warns. The local elite inherited their status, and the merchants required some amount of working capital in order to pursue profit. These roles, consequently, were unavailable to most inhabitants of agrarian cities. If one could not achieve the status of the landowners or the wealth of the merchants, though, more limited opportunities for social advancement remained available. Becoming a teacher was one such opportunity in the Jacobin churches. The passage implies that this role gave the incumbents an opportunity to display their verbal skills publicly. This privilege provided not only an opportunity to exhibit their learning and provide leadership in some matters but also a forum from which to preserve their status by disparaging their opponents. Using its implied analogy of a patronage system, the epistle argues that insiders of high status should not abuse other insiders verbally. All are clients of the same benefactor, so, regardless of one's position in the ecclesiastical pecking order, one directs verbal riposte more appropriately towards outsiders.

The criticism of verbal abuse culminates with 4:11-12. The utility of successful defamation in a game of challenge and riposte is self-evident. Only the possibility of retaliation in kind could provide a practical limit to the potential payoff.[40] The epistle downplays this pragmatic consideration and suggests that the strategy is inherently unethical. Successful defamation both constitutes a judgement against a person and accomplishes the consequent reduction of that person's status.[41] Since the privilege of judgement resides properly with the

---

[40]This possibility constituted the topic of a caveat with wide circulation in classical antiquity. See, for example, Quintilian, *Inst. Orat.*, 12:9:8-11, Matt. 5:11-12, Lucian of Samosata, "Professor of Public Speaking," 22-23 and "How to Write History," 8.

[41]Cf., R C. Webber, "'Why Were the Heathen so Arrogant?'" The Socio-Rhetorical Strategy of Acts 3-4," *Biblical Theology Bulletin*, 22/1 (spring, 1992), 20-21.

divine patron, a client's usurpation of this role constitutes a naked power grab, an example of impudence which the patron must punish.

James concludes by advocating the use of verbal methods both to enhance the condition of individual audience members and to honor the divine patron. Songs of praise, prayer, and confession clarify both the role of the congregants as clients and that of the deity as benefactor (5:13-16). The elders, who occupy a quasi-official position by virtue of their age, receive no criticism. This position is not easily susceptible to games of challenge and riposte. The example of Elijah demonstrates the utility of supplication which maintains the social distance between those of unequal status (vv. 17-18). Finally, the rehabilitation of a sinner constitutes an appropriate concern for the fellow client's status and a demonstration of concern for the group rather than for one's own prestige. On this topic, James and Paul express similar sentiments (vv. 20-21, cf., Gal. 6:1-5).

James, Paul, and Abraham

The preceding interpretation of James characterizes the epistle as invective against certain methods of social climbing. The epistle discourages the use of loyalty tests and games of challenge and riposte among insiders. Particularly insidious is the implication that the deity is open for testing by humans. Wisdom, likewise, is not an appropriate basis for a claim to status within the church. Christians receive divine wisdom as a grant from their benefactor and, in turn, demonstrate such wisdom by behaving in a manner which contributes to the collective well-being of the group within which they are embedded. Inherited and earned wealth, likewise, receive criticism. In a society characterized by limited good, both are attributed to abusive practices and thus do not warrant the validation of high status within the church. Finally, the epistle virtually equates verbal riposte with verbal abuse and encourages material support for disadvantaged constituents as a more appropriate direction in which to guide the patronal tendencies of the well-to-do and pretentious.

P. U. Maynard-Reid characterizes James as an attack upon the rich and a consolation for the poor and oppressed.[42] The survey above demonstrates the presence of this component. The epistle's agenda, however, covers a range of related topics wider than Maynard-Reid indicates. The epistle was written in an era in which social status was at least as important as was economic, and the two were not identical. Thus, it attributes wealth to abusive practices, in a manner consistent with the assumption of limited good, and incorporates this entire topic into a more comprehensive framework of social climbing in the Jacobin churches. Whether the listener is rich, influential for other reasons, or simply pretentious, the epistle warns that he is embedded in the group and must attend to the collective good rather than to his own status. Thus, the epistle speaks primarily to the Jacobin Christians who occupied or aspired to high status in order to warn them that all methods of increasing prestige and wealth carry divisive potential.

James bases its invective regarding social climbing upon a widely known but implicit social model. In the cities of classical antiquity, those with wealth could enhance their prestige by becoming patrons to the less fortunate. In return for a subsistence allowance, they could be attended in public by clients, have recourse to the services of literate personnel, and receive deference or veneration. The services which the patrons received from their clients provided the actual, public validation of the patrons' claims to increased status.

The epistle uses the prevalence of this model to discourage social climbing. It characterizes the Jacobin churches as a large patronage network. Within this network, all believers have the status of client. The deity stands alone as patron and benefactor to the churches. Consequently, the competition among clients for status on the pecking order is misplaced. Such contests not only prove divisive but desecrate the deity's unique status. As in the larger culture, insiders should initiate contests for honor not with other insiders but with representatives of other families, voluntary associations, and patronage networks.

Christian audiences of the first several centuries CE conformed James to Paul adequately to ensure the canonization of James. The faith-works dichotomy,

---

[42] *Poverty and Wealth in James* (Maryknoll, NY: Orbis, 1987), p. 97.

as illustrated by the example of Abraham, provides the most obvious basis of comparison. This dichotomy, however, served Paul's purposes primarily in Gal. and Rom., the epistles in which he treated the relationship of Gentile and Jewish Christians and non-Christian Jews. Paul apparently did not consider the dichotomy or the example useful in his treatment of socioeconomic questions in other epistles.

The survey above demonstrates an alternative method of conforming James to Paul. In keeping with the Jacobin emphasis, Abraham and the faith-works dichotomy recede in importance, along with the Pauline epistles in which they receive treatment. This chapter's hypothetical, post-Pauline audience reads James primarily in comparison with I Cor., the epistle in which Paul disparages internal cliques, intramural squabbles, socioeconomic divisions, and the competition for honor most severely. Both epistles utilize various sorts of corporate imagery, condemn verbal abuse, contrast divine wisdom with the use of wisdom for self-aggrandizement, and refuse to tolerate the use of economic methods to increase one's own prestige by belittling other insiders.

The example of Abraham illustrates the Jacobin insistence on proper deference to the divine benefactor. The epistle praises Abraham's works as epitomized by his obedience to the order to sacrifice his son (2:20-24). Rahab, likewise, is saved on account of her hospitality to the vulnerable Israelite spies (2:25). In ancient cultures, faith was tantamount to affiliation. One might, at least theoretically, encounter a needy individual, express the proper, pious sentiments, and thereby reinforce his status as an insider (2:17). Ethical participation in the Jacobin group, in contrast, requires works in accordance with one's status as a client of the deity. In other words, the the group must validate and the individual must obey the divinely sanctioned instructions regarding behavior towards the patron and other believers/clients. These instructions require behavior which not only relativizes the church's internal pecking order by classifying all constituents as clients but also mirrors the patron's generosity. James defines works in this sense and promises its compliant listeners vindication such as that which Abraham received for his obedience.

Chapter Four

EPILOGUE:
JAMES IN DIVERSE SETTINGS

The proposed, post-Pauline interpretation of James proves advantageous in several respects. First, it alleviates the adversarial aspects of reading strategy by reducing the gap between the author's cultural milieu and those of modern readers. By proposing a fictitious audience based on the agonistic characteristics common to many first century agrarian societies, it enables modern readers to place themselves figuratively in the shoes of their ancient, Mediterranean predecessors. This method includes a good measure of circular reasoning. Modern readers use data from James to illustrate Lenski's and Malina's models and to suggest similarities between the concerns of James and those of Paul. Subsequently, the same audiences use the comparable Pauline material and generalizations drawn from Lenski's and Malina's theories to intepret James. This technique leads inexorably to an emphasis upon the compatibility of the two sets of literature and two theoretical approaches but excludes readings which are undesirable by virtue of their predication solely on the assumptions and conditions of modern audiences.

The post-Pauline reading strategy also takes seriously the author's ground rules for interpretation. The interpretation begins with James' obviously epistolary framework and then uses topics found in James to define a choerent, though not tightly woven, progression of thought throughout the epistle. The generic identification of the letter as a circular epistle delivered in the hope that the earliest audiences would interpret it as a vehicle of authoritative instructions moves barely beyond the observations that the work has an epistolary framework and that it was preserved and ultimately canonized in spite of the surrounding controversy.

EPILOGUE

In summary, one may predicate the suggested, post-Pauline interpretation of James on three basic assumptions. First, the interpretation depends upon the lowest common denominator among assumptions regarding audience, authorial, and literary characteristics. Second, the proposition of a typical, urban, first century audience is the least problemmatical of several possibilities. Third, this reading strategy constitutes the closest possible approach to authorial intention or earliest audience response. The second and third assumptions remain hypothetical and undemonstrable due to the virtual absence of specific information about the author or any of the intended audiences. These assumptions remain tenable only because they are less speculative than are any of the alternatives.

From a literary perspective, the proposed, post-Pauline interpretation of James, in comparison with the other possibilities among modern reading strategies, poses relatively few problems. This equivocation normally would render the interpretation questionable. The historical fate of the epistle, however, buttresses the probability that some ancient audiences used similar reading strategies. During the first two centuries after it was written, the epistle apparently received narrower dissemination than did the mainstays of the Christian canon. The ante-Nicene writers may have quoted bits and pieces of the epistle but did not cite James to the extent that they did Paul or the gospels. Given the Pauline orientation of what became orthodox Christianity, the reasons for this equivocation are no mystery. The epistle treats the faith-works dichotomy and the example of Abraham in a manner foreign to Paul and exhibits no concern for the ethnoreligious issues of Gal. and Rom. In addition, the epistle's socioeconomic prescriptions and the conservatism of the deutero-Paulines and the pastorals seem largely incompatible.

The post-Pauline reading suggests two possible incentives for the epistle's ultimate acceptance. James diverged from Paul in numerous particulars. First, given the epistle's focus on its audiences' continuity with Judaism, its treatment of Abraham and the faith-works dichotomy, and the author's name, one should not be surprised that post-Pauline Christians ultimately identified the author with the James stereotyped in Gal. 2. They probably found this identification, though unproven, as plausible as any of the alternatives, and the identification ironically lent the epistle an air of authority comparable to that of the Pauline corpus. The supposed author did not represent post-Pauline Christianity, but later audiences could not denigrate his status as Jesus' brother and leader of the Jerusalem community. Second, the epistle's criticism of intramural power struggles and social climbing mirrors some prescriptions with which a post-Pauline audience might have been familiar due to the prominence of such invective in 1 Cor. Paul instructed the elite and pretentious among his Corinthian followers to make concessions to avoid offending Christians of lower status. James, likewise, reminded his church leaders that they were clients of the divine benefactor rather than patrons to whom other church members owed deference. James, in short, was susceptible to interpretation by means of comparison to the Pauline corpus. This hermeneutic contributed to the epistle's ultimate acceptance into the post-Pauline canon, with the similarities between James and 1 Cor. providing the consistency necessary to ensure the status of James in the face of the obvious differences between the Jacobin and the Pauline perspectives.

One wild card remains in the current consideration of James. It is remotely possible that the epistle arose in a cultural milieu either opposed to or unfamiliar with many of the Pauline precepts. In such a scenario, the epistle would have been disseminated not only among anti-Pauline or non-Pauline but also among post-Pauline Christians. The latter group then would have conformed James to its norms by focusing on the invective against the social climbing prevalent in its own cities. Thus, the post-Pauline *Sitz im Leben* suggested above would have been one of at least two molds which shaped different audiences' readings of the epistle. We turn now to a brief consideration of this possibility in terms of a hypothetical Palestinian Christian audience.

James in a Hypothetical, Palestinian Provenance

The extant literature provides little information about the contours of first century Palestinian faith and practice. Thus, the interpreter cannot elucidate this hypothetical audience's background as clearly as he can that of its post-Pauline counterpart. As a result, the description of the Christian audience relies heavily on information about the general, first century Palestinian milieu.

EPILOGUE

M. Hengel argued in a well-known work[1] that Hellenistic culture exerted a pervasive influence over the Palestinian social institutions during the periods of Ptolemaic/Seleucid and Roman hegemony. Primary sources indeed substantiate Hengel's thesis of cultural amalgamation. 1 Macc., for example, commences by interpreting the Hasmonean uprising as a proportionate response to Antiochus Epiphanes' violent attempts to enforce his cultural standards upon his Palestinian subjects. These attempts included the construction of a gymnasium in Jerusalem, apparently accompanied by the participants' voluntary cosmetic procedures to conceal the evidence of their circumcisions (vv. 14-15), the forcible replacement of Jewish with Greek laws and religious rituals (vv. 41-59), and, finally, the use of capital punishment to enforce the prohibition of circumcision (vv. 60-64). More than a century after the Hasmonean uprising, Herod visited Octavian at Actium, received confirmation of his royal authority, and commenced on a Roman-style building program throughout Palestine (*Bel. Jud.*, 1:386 ff). His subsequent erection of an image of an eagle over a temple gate incurred the wrath of some Jerusalem residents who considered themselves Torah-observant (*Bel. Jud.*, 1:648 ff). Still later, Josephus, who wrote for the benefit of Roman imperial patrons, labelled Caligula's attempt to erect statues of himself in the Jerusalem temple an abuse. At this point, Josephus described the Jewish resistance to the measure and attributed the avoidance of a crisis to the delaying tactics of the Roman general Petronius, followed by the timely assassination of Caligula (*Bel. Jud.*, 2:184-203). Finally, Josephus dated the outbreak of the abortive rebellion of 66 CE to the discontinuation of the temple sacrifice for the emperor and the refusal to accept gifts from foreigners (*Bel. Jud.*, 2:408-417). Neither the nationalistic author of 1 Macc. nor the Flavian client Josephus made any attempt to conceal either the influence of or the resistence to the common, Greco-Roman culture.

Economic exploitation provided a second possible reason for hostility towards foreign overlords. Herod's building program, noted above, required both capital and labor. The requirement of tribute, as practiced by both the Seleucids

---

[1]*Judaism and Hellenism: Studies in Their Encounter in Palestine During the Early Hellenistic Period*, tr. J. Bowden. London/Philadelphia: SCM/Fortress, 1974, 2 vols.

and the Romans, could provide money for a conqueror, leave the tributary too weak to finance a revolt, and symbolize the unequal relationship in a graphic manner (eg., 1 Macc. 1:1-4, 3:29-31, 8:1-7, 10:29-33, 15:30-31, 2 Macc. 4:28, 8:10, 8:36).[2] Whether or not the Romans exacted taxation in a punitive manner in Palestine before the major uprisings, a question which remains subject largely to opinion, the synoptics took a dim view of the practices of the tax collectors who expropriated the resources directly. This position, of course, is predictable in light of Lenski's agrarian model. The Jesus of the first gospel easily induced the tax collector Matthew to leave his station and subsequently received criticism for eating with tax collectors, whom he identified explicitly as sinners (Matt. 9:9-13). The Jesus of the third gospel, likewise, received criticism for his table fellowship with Zaccheus, Jericho's wealthy head tax collector (Lk. 19:1-10). That Zaccheus obtained some of his wealth by fraudulent means occasioned less surprise than his offer to use some of the wealth to make restitution (vv. 8-9).

That foreign cultural and economic domination could provide a reason for hostility in an agonistic society scarcely requires mention. 1 Macc. 1:39-40, using language which modern interpreters identify explicitly with agonistic perspectives, argued that Antiochus Epiphanes' measures provided an occasion for Jerusalem's dishonor and shame. 1QpH cols. 3, 6, 9 ridiculed the brutality of an admittedly effective occupying army, possibly the Romans in light of the reference to their worship of standards and weapons. 1QM proposed not only a military strategy to defeat the "Kittim" but also an emphasis on the ceremonial and cultural concerns which apparently received short shrift in some quarters. Finally, the abortive, large-scale rebellions of 66 and 135 CE provide evidence not only of the foreign influence in first century Palestine but also of the resistance which the influence engendered in the more nationalistic circles.

In summary, the Roman hegemony of the first century CE constitutes the paramount issue for our hypothetical Palestinian Christian audience. The synoptic apocalypse reflects a degree of hostility towards the Romans, even adopting the

---

[2]R. C. Webber, "An Analysis of Power in the Jerusalem Church in Acts," unpublished Ph.D. diss. (Louisville, KY: Southern Baptist Theological Seminary, 1989), pp. 148-150.

derogatory title, "desolating sacrilege," from Dan. 11:31 and 1 Macc. 1:54, possibly to compare Caligula's proposed statue in the temple with the earlier practices of Antiochus Epiphanes.[3] In addition, all four gospels include passion narratives in which both the local Jerusalem elite and the Roman procurator played pivotal roles. Christians who wished to emphasize the xenophobic aspects of their faith had at least equivocal support from the traditions underlying their gospels.

R. Eisenman's treatment of the Qumran literature illustrates some methods of interpretation which emphasize the xenophobic aspects of other Palestinian audiences. Eisenman presents this body of literature as a polemic against the Romans and their indigenous supporters rather than against the earlier Seleucid regime.[4] On the basis of excerpts from several Qumran writings and Josephus, he portrays Herod as a quisling who imported Hillel and Simon b. Boethus to sanction his conciliatory policy and then supported a pro-Roman aristocracy with the wealth which he had confiscated from the more nationalistic Hasmoneans after eradicating that family.[5] Consequently, the Qumran sectaries labelled the Pharisees and the Sadducees "seekers after smooth things" owing to the latter groups' preferences for pro-Roman policies and expedient measures to maintain the peace around Jerusalem (cf., Jn. 11:49-53).[6]

Eisenman interprets the Qumran community's concept of righteousness (*zedek*) in terms of xenophobia He attributes to the concept an esoteric connotation; the righteous priesthood is selected in the traditional manner, that is, by lot, rather than appointed by foreign overlords. Furthermore, descent from the

---

[3]G. Theissen, *The Gospels in Context: Social and Political History in the Synoptic Tradition*, tr. L. M. Maloney (Minneapolis: Fortress, 1991), pp .157-165.

[4]In this respect, Eisenman distinguishes his dating of the Qumran literature from that of the mainstream of scholarship. However, his disagreement over the date merely heightens the xenophobic aspects of the literature. Mainstream scholars, exemplified by B. Z. Wacholder (*The Dawn of Qumran: The Sectarian Torah and the Teacher of Righteousness* [Cincinnati, OH: Hebrew Union College, 1983], pp. 176 ff) note the xenophobic character of the literature as readily as does Eisenmann. They simply identify the objects of this xenophobia as the foreign overlords of earlier generations.

[5]*Maccabees, Zadokites, Christians and Qumran: A New Hypothesis of Qumran Origins* (SPB; Leiden: E. J. Brill, 1983), pp. 24-25.

[6]*Ibid.*, p. 36.

Solomonic high priest Zadok is a matter of limited concern.[7] Thus, Eisenman argues that the Qumran sectarians considered the Jerusalem priesthood and the dominant political parties illegitimate on the basis of their shared willingness to remain subservient to the Roman overlords. R. A. Rosenberg, like Eisenman, favors an esoteric interpretation of the concept of righteousness. In contrast with Eisenman, however, his interest lies in the possibility of a typological adaptation of this concept by Jesus and some of the NT authors.[8]

Eisenman identifies zeal for the law as a characteristic of the righteous priesthood.[9] In a later monograph, he notes that Jesus' brother James received acclaim for epitomizing this characteristic and then contrasts zeal for the law with Pauline antinomianism. Reading 1QpH in light of this contrast enables him to suggest that the pesher constitutes the Jerusalem Christian community's *post facto* response to the Jerusalem Council of Gal. 2/Acts 15. This interpretation casts 1QpH as an allegory in which the titles Teacher of Righteousness, Man of Lies, and Wicked Priest represent James, Paul, and Ananus respectively.[10] Thus, Eisenman posits the existence of an anti-Pauline tradition, associated intimately with Jesus' brother James, during the first two Christian generations.

In spite of its controversial reputation among Qumran specialists, Eisenman's reconstruction provides a provocative point of departure for the analysis of James. The existence of a version of Christian faith and practice associated with the name of James and unsympathetic to the perceived antinomianism of the Pauline alternative is highly probable. Paul himself made no secret of his quarrel with emissaries from Jesus' brother over the question of table fellowship between Jewish and Gentile Christians (Gal. 2:11-14). Acts, a work removed by some years from its subject matter, noted both James' status as head of the Jerusalem church and his interest in those Christians "zealous for the law" (21:17-26). The author of this work apparently suggested a level of accomodation

---

[7]*Maccabees, Zadokites, Christians and Qumran*, pp. 4-11

[8]*The Veneration of Divine Justice: The Dead Sea Scrolls and Christianity* (CSR 40; Westport, CT/London: Greenwood, 1995).

[9]*Ibid.*, pp. 10-16.

[10]*James the Just in the Habbakuk Pesher* (SPB; Leiden: E. J. Brill, 1986), pp. 24-42, 55-65.

between James and Paul, as he portrayed the former as a gracious host and the latter as a guest who downplayed his antinomian tendencies in order to protect the host's honor among his zealously legalistic constituents.

The attribution of the epistle of James to Jesus' brother, of course, cannot be sustained. However, the epistle's vague identification of its intended recipients allows the interpreter to read the epistle in light of an audience such as those which Paul and Acts may have associated with Jesus' brother. Eisenman's and Rosenberg's interpretations of some Qumran writings provide descriptive material to specify the nature of such an audience's legalism in much the same manner as the Pauline and post-Pauline epistles enable the modern reader to delineate the contours of the hypothetical post-Pauline audience. This legalism identifies the concept of righteousness as the definitive aspect of an alternative to the conforming and quietistic Pauline version of Christianity.

A Palestinian reading of James may avail itself of the same topical outline as did the preceding Pauline interpretation. The first chapter serves as a précis, introducing the topics of testing, wisdom, economic favoritism, and verbal riposte, all of which the subsequent chapters elaborate. The Pauline reading incorporates these topics into an heuristic framework informed by the general socioeconomic conditions of ancient Mediterranean cities. The Palestinian reading requires recourse not only to these conditions, which were as pervasive in Palestinian cities as they were elsewhere, but also to the resentment towards the conditions, which came to a head more frequently and violently than it did in most other areas under Roman imperial domination.

The introduction of testing identifies the solidification of the believer's group affiliation (ie., his faith) as a beneficial outcome of such difficult experience (1:2-4, 12). Since this particular affiliation presumably enjoys divine sanction, the proposition that the deity participates in the testing game becomes difficult to sustain (1:13-16). The deity, rather, provides an example of giving which the audiences are encouraged to imitate in order to bring divine righteousness to fruition (1:17-21). The desire for such righteousness precludes the expression of anger within the assembly of believers (1:19) and necessitates the humility which the epistle treats in more detail within the context of other topics.

EPILOGUE

The concepts of testing and righteousness become amenable to nationalistic understandings in an agonistic culture which equates faith primarily with affiliation. If James were to be read in a conflict-ridden, xenophobic context, one might interpret the passages on testing as sarcastic efforts to encourage the continued loyalty of the author's followers. One is tested not by the deity but by his own doubts in the face of difficult circumstances, such as those in Palestine during and after the revolt of 66-73 CE. The successful negotiation of such hardships solidifies corporate identity, embeddedness, and, thus, opposition to the invading forces, in spite of the futility of such resistance.

Testing, giving, and anger lead naturally to a discussion of salvific works (^camal). The epistle urges its listeners to care for the most vulnerable insiders (1:26-27) and then cites a lengthy counterexample of economic favoritism (2:1-7). The former, charitable example falls into the category of a work which promotes pure religion and the latter into that of impermissible discrimination. The epistle argues that this practice is tantamount to the partiality inherent in selective Torah observance (2:8-12). In a more positive vein, however, the use of mercy at the expense of judgement to inform the particulars of Torah observance transforms this necessity into the "law of freedom" (2:12-13). In this respect, testing and salvific works give the epistle a non-Pauline orientation at the very least.

The examples of Abraham and Rahab solidify the possible interpretations which become apparent when one tries to read the epistle in a non-Pauline manner. Abraham's willingness to sacrifice his son Isaac and Rahab's hospitality towards the Israelite spies (2:18-26) exemplify the concept of works of the law. The epistle attributes the salvation of these two OT characters to their works. Abraham antedated the Israelite people,--he was their mythical ancestor--and Rahab's affiliation lay with the pre-Israelite inhabitants of Jericho. Thus, faith, defined with an ancient emphasis on group affiliation, was of limited utility for these two examples, requiring consummation by means of appropriate works (2:22, 24, 26).

In a xenophobic setting, the reinforcement and demonstration of faith by means of works (2:18) functions in a manner analogous to the solidification of loyalty in the face of testing. One might demonstrate his commitment to the group by behaving loyally and following divinely sanctioned instructions, as did the author's two examples. Of course, the risk inherent in such behavior would be readily apparent to anybody familiar with the methods which the Romans utilized to ensure the compliance of the provincials with their regime.

Salvific knowledge (da^cat) serves as a close counterpart to faith and salvific works. The epistle identifies such knowledge initially, using the roughly equivalent wisdom terminology more characteristic of the Greek language, as a byproduct of faith (1:5-6). As in the Pauline interpretation, this commodity is available to believers in a relatively egalitarian manner, simply as a bequest from the divine patron. Such da^cat manifests itself in the ^camal enumerated in 2:17 (cf., 1QS 8:1-4) and results in the peaceful intra-group conditions of 2:18. In fact, the epistle connects these two characteristics of salvation explicitly in 2:13.

Such knowledge contrasts with accomodationist interpretive activity in xenophobic societies. Eisenman characterizes the Qumran literary corpus as a reaction to such activity by the Jerusalem political and religious leadership.[11] James, of course, critizes some of the same groups urban elite which the Qumran corpus criticizes and Josephus characterizes as respectable citizens. These groups display an impressive consistency with those of high status which Lenski's model suggests would benefit from cooperation with an occupying force.

The Qumran community employed several interchangable self-designations which referenced the concepts of poverty, humility (in the modern sense), and/or low socioeconomic status. Most of these self-designations equate the statuses noted above with righteousness or honor which the deity ascribed to the group. James' discouragement of economic favoritism mirrors this usage. The initial treatment of the economic theme suggests that the poor believer has been exalted and the rich humiliated by their shared mortality (1:9-11). In this respect, the current reading mirrors the Pauline emphasis. Owing to this straightforward proposal that socioeconomic differences have been leveled, the epistle criticizes preferential treatment of the wealthy in church assemblies as an impermissible sort of discrimination (1:1-7). Other Christian literature, of course, implies the use of such seating arrangements both in the Pauline churches' observances of the Lord's

---

[11] *Maccbees, Zadokites, Christians and Qumran*, p. 21.

Supper and in the conduct of meals and synagogue assemblies by the Matthean Jesus' opponents (cf., p. 83 above).

The argument in favor of the poor or humble continues with the scathing criticism of two wealthier classes. The epistle criticizes the wealthy merchants for exhibiting the arrogance previously contrasted with salvific wisdom (4:13-17) and then accuses the even wealthier landowners of withholding the wages of their hired labor (5:1-5). This latter accusation may mirror the vague reference of 1QpH 8:7-12 to the theft of wealth from brutal men and the embezzlement of public funds by the "Wicked Priest." The Qumran *pesher*, like James, threatens the perpetrator with divine retribution in the eschaton.

The zenith of the argument in favor of the poor and humble represents the reverse of the criticism of the two wealthier classes. The laborer killed by the fraudulent withholding of his subsistence wages is identified explicitly in 5:6 as the righteous one (*zaddik*). In a sectarian Jewish setting, this term carries extensive connotations regarding the salvific efficacy of the death of the *zaddik*, upon analogy with the activity of the protagonist of Is. 52-53.[12] Such a person might be called upon to die for the sake of his followers. Immediately thereafter, the epistle cites the subsistence farmer, a person of low socioeconomic status, as its initial example of perseverence until the eschaton (5:7-9). The prophets and Job, who resisted all manner of temptation, follow as prototypes of the righteous one whose activity exemplifies the Lord's mercy (5:10-11).

The criticism of the wealthy in James constitutes the reverse of Josephus' description of the beginning of hostilities in Jerusalem. According to this account, written from an upper-class perspective, the rebellious forces took advantage of a festival to burn the high priest's house and some palaces. After the inception of hostilities in this manner, they burned the archives in order to destroy the contracts and debt records which obligated the poorer inhabitants to pay their creditors. Josephus claims that this gesture brought into sharp relief the bifurcation of the Jerusalem population into wealthy accomodationists and poorer inhabitants who

---

[12]See Rosenberg, *Veneration of Divine Justice*, pp. 95-96 for a discussion of the Christian interpretation of Jesus' crucifixion in terms of this concept.

determined that their interests had become consistent with those of the rebellious forces (*Bel. Jud.*, 2:426-429). As Josephus denounced the populist behavior of the rebels in Jerusalem, so James criticizes the elitist behavior of his audiences' leaders. The two critiques, in other words, constitute opposite sides of the same coin. James examines economic mistreatment from the perspective of the underclass.[13] In this respect, the refusal to pay the typical wage for work performed provides a possible rationale for behavior such as that which Josephus described.

The epistle repeatedly condemns the use of verbal riposte in intramural squabbles. An introductory statement urges the listeners to speak and become angry deliberately and contrasts anger with the paramount quality of righteousness (1:19-21). The grave responsibility of the teaching role takes precedence over the high status which the incumbent might enjoy, and the irresponsible use of the tongue receives extended treatment (3:1-12). Perhaps the description in 1QpH of the behavior of the Teacher of Righteousness and the Man of Lies provides an analogy to the epistle's warnings, with the one mirroring the teacher's responsibility and the other the abuse of speech. Finally, 4:1-12 criticizes internal dissension and slander much as 1QpH 2:1-11 criticizes the treachery of the Man of Lies.

In summary, the hypothetical Palestinian reading of James both mirrors and counters various aspects of the hypothetical Pauline reading. The interpretations emphasize a similar range of topics due to the fact that the epistle includes these topics and makes them unavoidable. In this respect, as the social model of reading indicates, the author wields some influence over the subsequent interpretation of his work. The creative energy of the audiences begins where the specificity of the author ends. The post-Pauline audience finds ample material to support its reading of James as a brief epistle warning against the perils of social climbing. In this respect, the audience conforms James to Paul by reading it in comparison primarily with 1 Cor. The Palestinian audience, in contrast, treats James as a handbook on righteousness. This reading shares some of the tone of its Pauline counterpart; the two, after all, warn against some of the same evils.[14] However, the two readings

---

[13] Maynard-Reid, *Poverty and Wealth in James*, pp. 85-93.

[14] In addition, Rosenberg proposes sadoqite roots for some aspects of Paul's doctrine of justification (*Veneration of Divine Justice*, pp. 110-111).

part ways when the Pauline cites Abraham and Rahab as mere examples of proper behavior by a client, minimizing the mechanisms of their honor, and the Palestinian identifies them as the epitome of the righteous person's justification by works. The xenophobia of the hypothetical Palestinian reading provides an additional layer of differentiation while simultaneously demonstrating the pervasiveness of the common, Greco-Roman culture in that geographic area.

James in Canonical Context

The hypothetical, post-Pauline interpretation carries considerable support. It displays an internal consistency which the alternative reading lacks. In addition, its subject matter, when read in a straightforward manner, is consistent with the characteristics of the urban, agrarian societies of the eastern Mediterranean basin. In addition, the likely dissemination of James as a circular epistle reinforces the general, typical character of the exhortations read from a post-Pauline perspective. The hypothetical, Palestinian interpretation, in contrast, requires the reader to characterize James as a more highly veiled form of rhetoric. This reading elucidates some possible bases of comparison but serves largely as a foil to control the excesses of the post-Pauline perspective.

Ironically, post-Pauline Christians have preserved James in such a manner as to emphasize the inherent possibility of a Palestinian interpretation. The Paul vs. James debate, as it relates to the relationship between faith and works and the examples of Abraham and Rahab, has emphasized the divergent aspects of the two possible interpretations. When one has been indoctrinated in the Pauline version of Christianity, for which the doctrine of justification by grace through faith is of paramount importance, the Jacobin emphasis on works, using the same examples and terminology, seems foreign. It is no wonder that subsequent Christian audiences questioned the reliability, and even the Christian character, of James.

The post-Pauline reading of James reconciles the two by minimizing the importance of this central, markedly non-Pauline passage. By conforming James' instructions on economic and social difficulties to those which Paul provided in 1 Cor., the interpretation draws the audience into a consideration of the similarities between the two epistles. Perhaps this similarity, more immediately evident to ancient than to modern audiences, ensured James' place in the emerging Christian canon. In any case, the post-Pauline reading appears consistent not only with Paul's instructions but also with what is known of the socioeconomic conditions in ancient Mediterranean cities.

On the other hand, perhaps the possibility of open disagreement between Paul and James ensured the inclusion of diverse materials in the canon. The two apparently disagreed on the mechanisms of justification. However, they agreed on the necessity of justification, the primary examples of this activity, and its socioeconomic dimensions. The dissemination of both letters illustrates the give and take, and possibly even the open debate, inherent in Christianity's development in the years before doctrinal chasms and institutional development necessitated the promulgation and calcification of rigid doctrines.

WORKS CITED

Primary Sources

Aristotle. "Politics," in *Aristotle* (complete works), tr. H. Rackham. Loeb Classical Library (LCL); Cambridge, MA/London: Harvard Univ./William Heinemann, 1990, vol. 21 of 23.

Caius Cornelius Tacitus. *Annals*, tr. J. Jackson. Cambridge, MA/London: Harvard Univ./ William Heinemann, 1979-1981, 5 vols.

Clemens Romanus. "Opera Omnia," in *Patrologiæ Cursus Completus*, Series Græcæ, ed. J.-P. Migne. Paris: Typographi Brepols Editores Pontificii, 1857, v. 1, pp. 199-327.

Decimus Junius Juvenalis. *Satires*, tr. G. G. Ramsay. LCL; Cambridge, MA/London: Harvard Univ./William Heinemann, 1950.

Eusebius Pamphilii. *The Ecclesiastical History*, tr. K. Lake, J. E. L. Oulton, & H. J. Lawlor. LCL; Cambridge, MA/London: Harvard Univ./William Heinemann, 1926-1942, 2 vols.

Flavius Josephus. *Josephus* (complete works), tr. H. St. J. Thackeray & R. Marcus. LCL; London: William Heinemann/New York: G. P .Putnam's Sons, 1926-1965, 10 vols.

WORKS CITED

Gaius Petronius. *Satyricon,* tr. M. Heseltine, rev. E. H. Warmington. LCL; Cambridge, MA/London: Harvard Univ./William Heinemann, 1987.

Ioannis Stobaei Anthologium, ed. C. Wachsmuth & O. Hense. Berlin: Weidemann, 1884-1923. 4 vols.

Lucian of Samosata. *Lucian* (complete works), tr. A. M. Harmon, M. D. MacLeod, & K. Kilburn. LCL; Cambridge, MA/London: Harvard Univ./William Heinemann, 1925-1968, 7 vols. Essays cited individually in the text include the following: "Alexander the False Prophet" (v. 4, pp. 173-254), "How to Write History" (v. 6, pp. 2-73), "On Salaried Posts in Great Houses" (v. 3, pp. 412-481), and "A Professor of Public Speaking" (v. 4, pp. 133-172).

Lucius Annaeus Seneca, "On the Shortness of Life," *Moral Essays,* tr. J. W. Basore. LCL; Cambridge, MA/London: Harvard Univ./William Heinemann, 1979, v. 2, pp. 286-355.

Lucius Junius Moderatus Columella. *Rei Rusticae,* tr. H. B. Ash. LCL; Cambridge, MA/London: Harvard Univ./William Heinemann, 1948, 2 vols.

Marcus Porcius Cato. *De Agri Cultura,* and Marcus Terentius Varro, *Rerum Rusticarum* (combined ed.), tr. W. D. Hooper, rev. H. B. Ash. LCL; Cambridge, MA/London: Harvard Univ./William Heinemann, 1979.

Marcus Valerius Martialis. *Epigrams,* tr. W. C. A. Ker. LCL; Cambridge, MA/London: Harvard Univ./William Heinemann, 1943, 2 vols.

Mekilta de Rabbi-Ishmael, tr. J. Z. Lauterbach. Philadelphia: Jewish Publication Society of America, 1976, 3 vols.

Mishnah, tr. H. Danby. Oxford: Oxford Univ., 1933.

Novum Testamentum Graece, 27th ed., ed. B. & K. Aland, J. Karavidopoulos, C. M. Martini, & B. M. Metzger. Stuttgart: Deutsche Bibelgesellschaft, 1993.

Philo of Alexandria. *Philo* (complete works), tr. F. H. Colson, G. H. Whittaker, & R. Marcus. LCL; Cambridge, MA/London: Harvard Univ./William Heinemann, 1929-1953, 12 vols.

WORKS CITED

Phocylides (pseudonym). *Gnomai.* Text and translation in Van der Horst, P. W. *The Sentences of Pseudo-Phocylides with Introduction and Commentary.* Leiden: E. J. Brill, 1978.

Plutarch of Chaeroneia. "On the Love of Wealth." *Moralia,* tr. P. H. DeLacy & B. Einarson. LCL; Cambridge, MA/London: Harvard Univ./William Heinemann, 1984, v. 7, pp. 6-39.

Quintilianus, Marcus Fabius. *Institutio Oratoria,* tr. H. E. Butler. LCL; Cambridge, MA/ London: William Heinemann, 1953, 4 vols.

Septuagint Version of the Old Testament and Apocrypha. Grand Rapids, MI: Zondervan, 1975.

Strabo. *Geography,* tr. H. L. Jones. LCL; New York/London: G. P. Putnam's Sons/ William Heinemann, 1917-1932, 8 vols.

The Dead Sea Scrolls Translated: The Qumran Texts in English, tr. F. García Martínez, Eng. ed. W. G. E. Watson. Leiden/New York/Cologne: E. J. Brill, 1994.

Xenophon. *Oeconomicus,* tr. E. C. Marchant. LCL; Cambridge, MA/London: Harvard Univ/William Heinemann, 1979, 4 vols.

Secondary Sources

Achtemeier, P. *"Omne Verbum Sonat:* The New Testament and the Oral Environment of Late Western Antiquity." *Journal of Biblical Literature,* 109/1 (1990), 3-27.

Bailey, K. E. *Poet and Peasant* and *Through Peasant Eyes: A Literary-Cultural Approach to the Parables of Luke.* Grand Rapids, MI: William B. Eerdmans, 1976/1980, 2 vols. in 1 (combined edition).

Balch, D. L. "'... You Teach All the Jews ... to Forsake Moses, Telling Them Not to ... Observe the Customs' (Acts 21:21, cf. 6:14)." *SBL Seminar Papers,* 32 (1993), 369-383.

WORKS CITED

Berger, P. L. & Luckmann, T. *The Social Construction of Reality: A Treatise in the Sociology of Knowledge.* Garden City, NY: Doubleday, 1967.

Bleich, D. *Subjective Criticism.* Baltimore/London: Johns Hopkins Univ., 1978.

Church, C. *A Forschungsgeschichte on the Literary Character of the Epistle of James.* Unpublished Ph.D. diss., Southern Baptist Theological Seminary, Louisville, KY, 1990.

Condon, G. "The Return of Huckleberry Finn." Louisville, KY *Courier-Journal*, 4/20/96, A15.

Crosman, R. "Do Readers Make Meaning?" S. R. Suleiman & I. Crosman, eds., *The Reader in the Text: Essays on Audience and Interpretation.* Princeton, NJ: Princeton Univ., 1980, pp. 149-164.

Davids, P.H. *The Epistle of James: A Commentary on the Greek Text.* NIGTC; Grand Rapids: William B. Eerdmans, 1982.

Davies, W. D. *Paul and Rabbinic Judaism: Some Rabbinic Elements in Pauline Theology*, 2nd ed. London: SPCK, 1955.

Deissmann, G. A. *Licht von Osten: Das Neue Testament und die neuentdeckten Texte der hellenistisch-römischen Welt*, 4en aufl. Tübingen: J. C. B. Mohr (Paul Siebeck), 1923.

Dibelius, M. *Der Brief des Jakobus.* KEKNT; Göttingen: Vandenhoeck & Ruprecht, 1921. (Tenth ed. in English as *A Commentary on the Epistle of James*, rev. H. Greeven, tr. M. A. Williams. Hermeneia; Philadelphia: Fortress, 1975.)

Donker, C. E. "Der Verfasser des Jakobus und sein Gegner: Zum Problem des Einwandes in Jak. 2,18-19." *Zeitschrift für die Neutestamentliche Wissenschaft und die Kunde der Älteren Kirche*, 72 (1981), 227-240.

Eisenman, R. *James the Just in the Habbakuk Pesher.* SPB; Leiden: E. J. Brill, 1986.

_____. *Maccabees, Zadokites, Christians, and Qumran: A New Hypothesis of Qumran Origins.* SPB; Leiden: E. J. Brill, 1983.

WORKS CITED

Finley, M. I. *The Ancient Economy.* Sather Classical Lectures 43; Berkeley/Los Angeles: Univ. of California 1973.

Goodman, M. *State and Society in Roman Galilee, A.D. 132-212.* Totowa, NJ: Rowman & Allanheld, 1982.

Hellholm, D. "The Problem of Apocalyptic Genre and the Apocalypse of John." *Semeia: An Experimental Journal for Biblical Criticism,* 36 (1979), 13-64.

Hengel, M. "Der Jakobusbrief als antipaulinische Polemik." *Tradition and Interpretation in the New Testament: Essays in Honor of E. Earle Ellis for His Sixtieth Birthday,* ed. G. F. Hawthorne & O. Betz. Grand Rapids, MI/Tübingen: William B. Eerdmans/J. C. B. Mohr (Paul Siebeck), 1987, pp. 248-278.

_____. *Judaism and Hellenism: Studies in Their Encounter in Palestine During the Early Hellenistic Period,* tr. J. Bowden. London/Philadelphia: SCM/Fortress, 1974, 2 vols.

Herzfeld, M. "'As in Your Own House': Hospitality, Ethnography, and the Stereotype of Mediterranean Society." *Honor and Shame and the Unity of the Mediterranean,* ed. D. D. Gilmore. Washington DC: Americal Anthropological Association, 1987, pp. 75-89.

Hirsch, E. D., Jr. *Validity in Interpretation.* New York/London: Yale Univ., 1967.

Iser, W. *The Act of Reading: A Theory of Aesthetic Response.* Baltimore/London: Johns Hopkins Univ., 1978.

Jameson, F. *The Political Unconscious: Narrative as a Socially Symbolic Act.* Ithaca, NY: Cornell Univ., 1981.

Johnson, L. T. *The Letter of James.* Anchor Bible 37A; NewYork/London/ Toronto/Sydney/Auckland: Doubleday, 1995.

Kent, T. L. *Interpretation and Genre: The Role of Generic Perception in the Study of Narrative Texts.* Lewisburg, PA: Bucknell Univ., 1986.

Laws, S. *The Epistle of James.* BNTC; Peabody, MA: Hendrickson, 1980.

113

Leenhardt, J. "Towards a Sociology of Reading," tr. B. Navelett & S. R. Suleiman. *The Reader in the Text: Essays on Audience and Interpretation,* ed. S. R. Suleiman & I. Crosman. Princeton, NJ: Princeton Univ., 1980.

Lenski, G. E. *Power and Privilege: A Theory of Social Stratification.* Chapel Hill, NC/London: Univ. of North Carolina, 1984.

Linton, G. "Reading the Apocalypse as an Apocalypse." *SBL Seminar Papers,* 30 (1991), 161-186.

Malina, B. J. *The New Testament World: Insights from Cultural Anthropology.* Atlanta: John Knox, 1981.

Mannheim, K. *Ideology and Utopia: An Introduction to the Sociology of Knowledge,* tr. L. Wirth & E. Shils. San Diego/New York/London: Harcourt Brace Jovanovich, 1936.

Martin, D. B. *Slavery as Salvation: The Metaphor of Slavery in Pauline Christianity.* New Haven, CT/London: Yale Univ., 1990.

Matthews, V. H. "Hospitality and Hostility in Genesis 19 and Judges 19." *Biblical Theology Bulletin,* 22/1 (spring, 1992), 3-11.

Maynard-Reid, P. U. *Poverty and Wealth in James.* Maryknoll, NY: Orbis, 1987.

Mayor, J. B. *The Epistle of James,* 2nd ed. London/New York: MacMillan, 1897.

Mussner, F. *Der Jakobusbrief.* HTKNT; Freiburg/Basel/Wein: Herder, 1964.

Piaget, J. *Biology and Knowledge,* tr. B. Walsh. Edinburgh: Edinburgh Univ., 1971.

Pitt-Rivers, J. *The Fate of Shechem or the Politics of Sex: Essays in the Anthropology of the Mediterranean.* Cambridge/London/Melbourne/New York: Cambridge Univ., 1977).

Perdue, L. "Paraenesis and the Epistle of James," *Zeitschrift für die Neutestamentliche Wissenschaft und die Kunde der Älteren Kirche,* 72 (1981), 241-256.

WORKS CITED

Ropes, J. H. *A Critical and Exegetical Commentary on the Epistle of St. James.* ICC; Edinburgh: T. & T. Clark, 1916.

Rosenberg, R. *The Veneration of Divine Justice: The Dead Sea Scrolls an Christianity.* CSR 40; Wesport, CT/London: Greenwood, 1995.

Ste. Croix, G. E. M. de *The Class Struggle in the Ancient Greek World from the Archaic World to the Arab Conquest.* Ithaca, NY: Cornell Univ., 1981.

Sanders, E. P. *Paul and Palestinian Judaism: A Comparison of Patterns of Religion.* Minneapolis: Fortress, 1977.

Siker, J. S. *Disinheriting the Jews: Paul in Early Christian Controversy.* Louisville, KY: Westminster/John Knox, 1991.

Theissen, G. *Studien zur Soziologie des Urchristentums*, 2er aufl. Tübingen: J. C. B. Mohr (Paul Siebeck), 1983. Essays cited individually in the text include the following: "Theoretische Probleme religionssoziologischer Forschung und die Analyse des Urchristentums" (pp. 55-76), "Soziale Schichtung in der Korinthischen Gemeinde: Ein Beitrag zur Soziologie des hellenistischen Urchristentums" (pp. 231-271), "Die Starken und Schwachen in Korinth: Soziologische Analyse eines theologischen Streites" (pp. 272-289), "Soziale Integration und sakramentales Handeln: Eine Analyse von 1 Cor. 11:17-34" (pp. 290-317), and "Christologie und soziale Erfahrung: Wissenssoziologische Aspekte paulinischer Christologie" (pp. 318-330).

_____. *The Gospels in Context: Social and Political History in the Synoptic Tradition*, tr. L. M. Maloney. Minneapolis: Fortress, 1991.

Thurén, L. "Risky Rhetoric in James?" *Novum Testamentum*, 37/3 (July, 1995), 262-284.

Trocmé, E. "Les Églises Pauliniennes vues du Dehors: Jacques 2,1 à 3,13." *Studia Evangelica*, 2 (1964), 660-669.

Verner, D. C. *The Household of God: The Social World of the Pastoral Epistles.* SBLDS 71; Chico, CA: Scholars, 1983.

Wacholder, B. Z. *The Dawn of Qumran: The Sectarian Torah and the Teacher of Righteousness.* Cincinnati, OH: Hebrew Union College, 1983.

Webber, R. C. "An Analysis of Power in the Jerusalem Church in Acts." Louisville, KY: Unpublished Ph.D. Diss. (Southern Baptist Theological Seminary), 1989.

_____. "Recent United States-Relations in Light of Traditional Near Eastern Cultural Norms." *Explorations: Journal for Adventurous Thought*, 10/2 (summer, 1992), 45-66.

_____. "The Apocalypse as Utopia: Ancient and Modern Subjectivity." *SBL Seminar Papers*, 32 (1993), 104-118.

_____. "'Why Were the Heathen So Arrogant?' The Socio-Rhetorical Strategy of Acts 3-4." *Biblical Theology Bulletin*, 22/1 (spring, 1992), 19-25.

Weber, M. *Economy and Society: An Outline of Interpretive Sociology*, ed. & tr. G. Roth, C. Wittich, et al. Berkeley/Los Angeles/London: Univ. of California, 1978. 2 vols.

INDEX OF ANCIENT SOURCES

APOCRYPHA

1 Maccabees

1:1-4	99
1:14-15	98
1:39-40	99
1:41-59	98
1:54	100
1:60-64	98
2:52	68
3:29-31	99
8:1-7	99
10:29-33	99
15:30-31	99

2 Maccabees

4:28	99
8:10	99
8:36	99

Judith

8:25-27	68

Wisdom of Sirach

34:21-22	86
44:20	26

ARISTOTLE

Politeia

1:2:23	36

CATO

De Agri Cultura

5:1-5	36

COLUMELLA

Rei Rusticae

1:8:2-6	36

EUSEBIUS

Ecclesiastical History

3:39:14-17	2
3:23-25	1

1 CLEMENT

13:1	75
38:5	75

JOHN STOBAEUS

Anthologeium 73

FLAVIUS JOSEPHUS

Bellum Judaeorum

1:386 ff	98
1:648 ff	98
2:184-203	98
2:408-417	98
2:426-429	106

Vita 1:1-6 37

JUVENAL

Satires

5	76, 80
7	76
9	76

LUCIAN OF SAMOSATA
Alexander the False Prophet 81
How to Write History 91
On Salaried Posts 76, 77, 80
Prof. of Public Speaking 91

MARTIAL
Epigrams
    1:20   81
    1:59   76
    1:101   76

MEKILTA
Beshallah
    7:141   28
    7:142-144 28

MISHNAH
Aboth 5:3   27
    5:3   27
Kiddushin
    4:14   27

NEW TESTAMENT
Matthew
    1:1-17   37
    4:1   68
    5:11-12 91
    6:13   68
    9:9-13   99
    16:1   68
    19:3   68
    20:1-16 46, 86
    22:13   84
    22:18   68
    22:35   68
    22:40   2
    ch. 23   5
    23:6   83
    26:17-30 83

Mark
    1:13   68
    7:1-13   2
    8:1-11   68
    10:2   68
    12:15   68
    12:18-34 2
    14:12-26 83
    14:38   68
Luke 3:23-38 37
    4:2   68
    4:13   68
    4:14-21 83
    8:13   68
    10:25-28 2
    11:4   77
    11:16   68
    14:12-14 77
    18:18-23 2
    19:1-10 99
    19:8-9   99
    20:23   68
    22:7-38 83
    22:28   68
    22:40   68
John ch. 9   100
    11:49-53 5
Acts 5:1-7 90
    6:1-7   76, 77
    ch. 15 11, 33
    ch. 18 64
    ch. 21 33
    21:17-26 101
Romans
    1:1   35
    ch. 4   29
    4:3   23, 62
    11:1   37
    11:28-36 75

INDEX OF ANCIENT SOURCES

First Corinthians

chs. 1-2	79
chs. 1-3	74
1:10-17	36
1:10-28	88
1:17	74
1:18	74
1:19	74
1:20	74
1:21-31	74
1:26	75
1:26-28	75
1:29	88
1:29-31	75
1:31	88
2:5	74
2:8	75
2:13	75
2:14	74
3:1-20	88
3:10-15	1, 88
3:22-23	88
7:5	68
ch. 9	36
9:17	36
ch. 10	71
10:6, 11-12	68
10:9	68
10:13	68
11:17-34	80
11:21-22	80
11:33-34	80
11:34	83
12:1-11	88
12:12-16	89
12:12-31	83
12:22-24	89
12:27-31	89

Second Corinthians

1:12	75
11:15	89

Second Corinthians (cont'd)

11:7-15	89
11:23-29	89
11:30-12:10	89
13:5	68

Galatians

ch. 2	11
2:9-13	33
2:11-14	81, 101
ch. 3	29
3:1-25	61
3:6	23
6:1-5	92
6:2	68
6:4-5	68

Ephesians

1:8, 17	75
3:10	75

Philippians

1:1	35
1:3-8	83
2:6-11	89
2:14	90
3:4-6	37
3:7-11	90

Colossians

1:9	75
1:28	75
2:3	75
2:23	75
3:16	75
4:5	75

First Thessalonians

1:2-10	83
ch. 3	68

Second Thessalonians

3:6-13	73

First Timothy

3:3-5	68
3:5	68
3:6-10	68

Titus	1:1	35	*James (cont'd)*	
Hebrews			2:8-12	103
	ch. 11	28	2:12-13	85, 103
	11:8-19	27	2:13	104
	11:31	27	2:14-26	23
James	1:1	16, 31, 33	2:17	94, 104
	1:1-7	104	2:18	103, 104
	1:2	70	2:18-26	103
	1:2-4, 12	102	2:19	26
	1:2-8	40	2:20-24	94
	1:3-4	70	2:21-22	23
	1:5	77	2:22, 24, 26	103
	1:5-6	104	2:25	27, 94
	1:5-8	77	ch. 3	55
	1:9 ff	54	3:1	90
	1:9-10	82	3:1-2	90, 106
	1:9-11	87, 104	3:1-18	40, 42
	1:9-18	40, 41	3:3-8	91
	1:11	82	3:9-12	91
	1:12-15	67, 71	3:13-17	76
	1:13-16	102	3:13-18	77, 79
	1:16-17	82	3:15-16	79
	1:17-21	102	3:17	79
	1:19	102	3:17-18	79
	1:19-20	90	ch. 4	55
	1:19-21	106	4:1-10	40, 41
	1:19-27	40, 42, 90	4:1-12	106
	1:22	42	4:11-12	40, 42, 91
	1:24	67	4:13-17	40, 42, 54, 85,
	1:25	90		86, 105
	1:26	90	4:13-5:6	87
	1:26-27	103	4:13-5:11	41
	1:27	90	5:1-5	105
	ch. 2	28, 29	5:1-6	85, 86
	2:1 ff	54	5:3-4	87
	2:1-7	84, 103	5:7	55
	2:1-13	83	5:7-9	105
	2:1-26	40, 41	5:7-11	68, 72
	2:2	83, 84	5:10-11	105
	2:6-7	41, 55, 84	5:12	40
	2:8	84	5:13-16	92

INDEX OF ANCIENT SOURCES

James (cont'd)
5:13-18	40, 42
5:14	55
5:17-18	92
5:19-20	40
5:20	96

Second Peter
1:1	35
3:14-16	2
Jude 1:1	35

Revelation
1:1	35
6:5-6	86
18:11-18	86
19:11-19	86

OLD TESTAMENT

Genesis
12:1	26
15:6	23, 26, 27, 28
	61, 62, 64, 65
22:1	68
26:5	26, 27, 28

Exodus
17:2	68
20:20	23

Numbers
14:22	68

Deuteronomy
8:2	68
Judges 2:22	68

1 Chronicles
1:7-13	78

1 Kings
3:3-14	78
Isaiah 7:12	68
29:14	74
chs. 52-53	105
Daniel 11:31	100

PETRONIUS
Satyricon
29 ff	84
29-30	36
32	84

PHILO OF ALEXANDRIA
De Abrahamo
273-276	26

De Migratione Abrahami
(passim)	26

De Virtutibus
214-216	26

Legum Allegoriae
3:228	26

Quod Deus Immutabilis Sit
3-4	26

Quis Rerum Divinarum Heres
90-93	26

PLUTARCH OF CHAERONEIA
Moralia 527D	84

PSEUDO-PHOCYLIDES
Sentences
19	86
116-121	82

QUINTILIAN
Institutio Oratoria
12:9:8-11	91

QUMRAN
Community Rule (1QS)
8:1-4	104

Habbakuk pesher (1QpH)
passim	101
2:1-11	106
cols. 3, 6, 9	99
8:7-12	105

QUMRAN (cont'd)
War scroll (1QM)   99

SENECA
De Brevitate Vitae   82

STRABO
Geography
         14:2:5   76, 90

TACITUS
Annals 1:2   76, 90

VARRO
Rerum Rusticarum
         1:17:1-1:18:4 36

XENOPHON
Oeconomicus 5:16   36

GENERAL INDEX

ᶜ*amal*   103-104
Abraham, example of   22-29, 61-62, 64-66, 92, 94, 96, 107
academic environment   19-21
agonism   48-49, 69-71, 79, 87, 99
agrarian societies   44-49, 73, 87
Ananus (high priest)   101
Antilochus   3
Antioch on the Orontes   82
Antiochus Epiphanes   98, 100
apatheia   74
Apollos   88
Aristotle   74
artisans, urban   73
Athanasius   3
Augustine of Hippo   3
Augustus (Octavian)   76, 98
authorial intention   9, 38-39, 96
Bailey, K. E.   48
banquets   80-81, 84
baptism, Christian   75
Bar Kochba revolt   4
Berger, P.   6
Bleich, D. L.   11-12
Bultmann, R. K.   20
Bush, G. H. W.   53
Caligula   98, 100
canonization, Christian   3, 5, 12, 108
canonization, Jewish   4-5

challenge and riposte   52, 71-72, 89-92, 97
Church, C.   9, 16
Claudius   81
Clement, bp. of Rome   75, 81
conceptual hierarchicalization   15
Corinth, Pauline church in   62-64, 73-74, 88-89, 107-108
covenantal nomism   61
Crosman, R.   9
Cynics   74
Cyril of Jerusalem   3
daᶜat   104
Davids, P. H.   21-22, 24-25, 33
defensive strategy   50
Dibelius, M.   16-21, 34, 56
Ebionism   57
Eisenman, R.   102-104, 106
Eusebius   1-2
faith vs. works   1, 22-29, 93, 96, 103-104, 107
genre, literary   13-14
governing classes   45, 55-56
halakah   4-5, 12
Hellholm, D.   15
Hengel, M.   23-25, 98
Herod the Great   98, 100
Herzfeld, M.   52
Hillel   100

Hirsch, E. D., Jr.   9
honor   51-52, 70-71, 79, 84
Huckleberry Finn, Adventures of   9
Hussein, S.   48, 53
Iser, W.   7
Ishmael b. Elisha, R.   27-28
James, audiences   57-59, 65-67,
      96-102, 106-108
James, authorship   16-22, 31, 33-38
James, epistolary framework   37-39, 95
James, Jesus' brother   17, 29, 33-34,
      82, 101-102
James, *Sitz im Leben*   18, 31, 40, 54, 97
James, textual criticism   7
Jameson, F.   9, 13, 39
Jerome   3
Jesus of Nazareth   69, 99
Job, example of   68, 72
John (Jerusalem church leader)   82
Johnson, L. T.   33, 67, 90
Josephus, Flavius   98, 100, 105-106
Joyce, W.   12
Judaism, pharasaic   3, 100
Juvenalis, D. Junius   76-77, 80
Kent, T. L.   14
landowners, wealthy   55, 85-88
Laws, S.   34
Leenhardt, J.   10
leisure   73
Lenski, G. E.   44-49, 63, 73,
      85, 95
limited good   47, 50
Linton, G.   13
litigation   84
Lord's Supper   63-64, 80-81
Lucian of Samosata   76-77, 80,
      81, 91
Luckmann, T.   6
Luther, M.   1
Malina, B. J.   49, 63, 69-70,
      79, 95

Mannheim, K.   6
Marcus Aurelius   74
Martialis, M. Valerius   76, 80-81
masoretic text   4
Matthews, V. H.   52
Maynard-Reid, P. U.   93, 106
Mayor, J. B.   2-3, 16-18, 20-21
Mekilta   32
merchants, wealthy   46, 55, 85-88
Mishnah   4-5, 27-28
Mussner, F.   22
Nehorai, R.   27-29
Origen of Alexandria   2, 5
Palestine, foreign hegemonies
      98-100
Palestine, taxation   99
Papias   2
patronage   64, 76-79, 83, 89, 93
Paul of Tarsus   22, 28, 29, 36, 57,
      61-62, 80-81, 89-90, 92,
      94, 101-102
perseverence   67-73
Persian Gulf War   52-53
Peter (Cephas)   81-82, 88
Petronius   84
Pharisees, see *Judaism, pharasaic*
Philo of Alexandria   25-29
Phocylides (pseud.)   82, 86
Piaget, J.   11
Pitt-Rivers, J.   51
Plato   74
Pound, E.   9-10
prophets, examples of   68, 71
Quintilianus, M. Fabius   91
Qumran   12, 100-102, 104, 106
Rahab, example of   27, 94, 107
reading, communal aspects of   110
reading, social model of   3-15,
      31-32, 106
retainer class   46
Revelation (NT book)   8, 86

righteousness (*zedek*)   100, 102, 105
rituals   1
Ropes, J. H.   16-21, 34
Rosenberg, R. A.   101-102, 105-106
Sadducees   100
Sanders, E. P.   60-61, 64
Schmidt, K. L.   20
Seneca, L. Annaeus   82
Septuagint   2, 23-24, 36, 69
shame   51, 84
Siker, J. S.   62
Simon b. Boethus   100
slavery, literary convention of
    35-36, 38, 89
social construction   6-7
socioeconomic distinctions   40-42
    45, 49, 54-56, 62-65
    73-75, 80-87, 104, 107-108
Solomon (ruler of united kingdom)   78

Stobaeus, John   73
Strabo   76, 90
subsistence farmers   68, 71, 73
synagogues   83
Tacitus, L. Cornelius   76, 90
Talmuds   4
tannaim   3-5
testing   67-73, 102-104
Theissen, G.   62-64, 81, 100
Trocmé, E.   34
twelve tribes   37-38
verbal riposte   42, 67, 86-92, 106
Wachholder, B. Z.   100
wealth   69, 77, 82, 93
Webber, R. C.   48, 50, 53, 78
    91, 99
Weber, M.   47
wisdom   67, 73-80
Zadok (high priest)   101